Calm Your Emotions:

Overcome Your Anxious, Negative, and Pessimistic Brain and Find Balance, Resilience, & Calm

by Nick Trenton
Nicktrenton.com

Table of Contents

CHAPTER 1. OUR VOLATILE EMOTIONS AND WHY THEY REIGN SUPREME — 7

EMOTIONAL ORIGINS — 11
THE PURPOSE OF EMOTIONS — 22

CHAPTER 2. THE KEYS TO ELIMINATING EMOTIONAL TRIGGERS — 31

THE NATURE OF TRIGGERS — 37
EMOTIONAL *NEEDS* — 42
THE EMOTIONAL SPECTRUM — 46

CHAPTER 3. RECOGNIZE, RESPOND TO, AND REGULATE THE CHAOS IN YOUR BRAIN — 55

A REGULATION FRAMEWORK — 61
DISTRESS TOLERANCE — 70

CHAPTER 4. FIGURING OUT AND REPLACING YOUR EMOTIONAL PATTERNS — 85

THE ABC LOOP — 87
EMOTIONAL DASHBOARDING — 96
THREE-STEP COGNITIVE BEHAVIORAL THERAPY — 102

CHAPTER 5. THE EMOTIONAL IMMUNE SYSTEM — 133

MIND GAMES — 139
THE SELF-ESTEEM CYCLE — 147

CHAPTER 6. PREVENTATIVE CARE — 163

WRITE IT OUT — 165
BRAIN DUMPING, MENTAL NOTING, AND SCHEDULED WORRY TIME — 173
BOUNDARY DEFENSE — 185

SUMMARY GUIDE — 195

Chapter 1. Our Volatile Emotions and Why They Reign Supreme

Though I wasn't the best student in school, I was able to develop a close friendship with my high school English teacher, Mr. Locke.

I'm not sure why he took an interest in me, but I suppose a convenient narrative is that he's the reason I ended up as a writer, and I have him to thank for all of it. Unfortunately, that would be false to say, as it's not remotely what we talked about most of the time.

Throughout the whole year, it was enlightening to ask him about the books we were reading for class and what he *actually* thought about them. *The Adventures of Tom Sawyer*? Overrated. *The Great Gatsby*? His favorite of all time. *Of Mice and Men*? He preferred the movie.

However, things got really interesting when the end of the year drew close and he started to open up about the people in my class—my peers. Of course, this was a dream come true for me: an adult willing to gossip with me about my fellow students. Looking back, it was wildly inappropriate for Mr. Locke to engage in such topics with me, but it's not like the teachers weren't doing it amongst themselves, anyway.

He let me in on a little secret of his: Whenever he had to give negative feedback, he would always make sure to try to build up the individual student a couple days before. He would do this to make sure their self-esteem, at least in the realm of his class, was sufficiently high, such that his negative feedback wouldn't have as big of an impact. He wanted students to not take things so personally and to be able to separate his comments on their work from them as a person. Too many students in the past had received his feedback in less than ideal ways. He wanted them to hear, "This paper could use work," not "*You* need work."

My teenage mind was blown away, and I told him that he was so clever to use "Jedi mind tricks" on his students. He told me there were a few students he would do this on more than others because he felt they had low self-esteem or he knew they were being bullied outside of his class. My adult mind still admires him and thinks that he had tremendous insight into how people worked—especially future adults who were still figuring themselves out and had fragile egos. It wasn't until much later that I realized he was helping students gain emotional resilience through raising their self-esteem.

Self-esteem is an essential component of emotional resilience and is often deemed *the immune system of emotions*. When it's high, you can handle what's thrown your way, and when it's low, you are more likely to collapse under scrutiny. Mr. Locke had somehow dialed into that and instilled that into his students.

Emotional resilience is a trait that is like the background music in a movie. When it's there, you don't notice it and it seems that scenes just fit together without a hitch. However, if it's missing, suddenly words are taken the wrong way, everything feels wrong, and the scene falls apart. In other words, you notice it when you need it, but not when you don't.

Therein lies the conundrum of resilience, emotional stability, and strength in the face of tragedy and despair—how do you get it before you need it, and how do you know if you don't have it? The ugly truth is that none of us are naturally born with it. Some of us are put into nasty situations where we develop coping mechanisms for strength, but that doesn't mean you are resilient. It just means the dam hasn't broken yet. And what will you do when the dam breaks?

My hope for this book is to arm you, whoever you are and whatever you may or may not have suffered, with tools and techniques to persevere and thrive. Emotional resilience is one of those rare qualities that cause a drastic shift in how you see the world. More importantly, it allows you to see *you* and gain better self-awareness of your thought patterns and behaviors. First understanding and then being able to harness and master your emotions gives you a lens of safety and control over the world, which gives you the feeling of being able to do anything.

Emotions are a major part of our existence and our identity as humans. Yet we don't often take a moment to think about where they come from, what they mean, why we feel certain ways, and how emotion actually affects us.

Why did I cry at that movie?

Because it was sad.

But why did I cry?

Because that's what you do when you're sad.

But . . . why?

We just accept that we are affected and don't take the time to think about how to strengthen or regulate certain emotions for our greater well-being. Unfortunately, it's this lack of attention that leads precisely to a lack of resilience. If you don't understand the forces at work inside your brain, you can only fall prey to them with no hope of regulating or even combating them. As such, we are completely at the whims of our emotional brain.

Mastering and conquering our emotional brains requires a bit of knowledge and background into what you are going to be battling. How do emotions function, what is their role, and why are they capable of completely dictating our lives?

Emotional Origins

What makes us feel emotions? How do we know and understand what we feel and *why* we feel it? If you were to ask one hundred people to answer those questions, you would probably get one hundred answers (let's be honest, you'd probably get more than one hundred!). Ultimately, it boils down to a study in neuroscience, but we will first explore two standard theories to explain the emotions that color our lives.

The first theory is called the *cognitive appraisal theory*, put forth by Swiss psychologist Klaus Scherer.

This theory states that emotions are judgments about the extent that a current situation meets your expectations and goals, no matter how you define them. Happiness is felt because it is an evaluation that your expectations are being met or even exceeded. If you win the lottery, you feel happiness because it solves your financial needs and likely exceeds your expectations. Similarly, if you receive a nasty unexpected bill in the mail, you also feel emotion—surprise and disappointment—since you almost certainly didn't wake up that morning expecting that to happen.

If you're asked out on a date, you feel happiness because it holds the promise of satisfying your romantic needs. In the same way, when you feel sadness, it is an evaluation that your goals are not being met or that the situation falls below your expectations, and anger might be the feeling that is aimed at whatever is blocking your goals.

Here, emotions are an instinctual reaction to objects or situations that relate to your expectations and goals. Often our goals are not clearly defined, as they can be both subconscious and conscious. You may not be able to say exactly why you're happy or disappointed at times—this theory sheds light on the fact that you subconsciously held some type of expectation that was or was not met.

If you are unemployed and presented with a job offer, you will feel happiness because you see it as a way to solve your financial worries. Alternatively, if you lose your job, you are saddened because you lose your financial stability. Your emotions are tied to how your status quo changes—another way we hold expectations we don't realize. In some cases, it may have little to do with the situation itself; maybe you've always hated your job and wanted to leave it. But when you're faced with the unexpected loss, you are saddened because it represents the loss of stability and your future career.

I had a friend who sometimes liked to toss a coin to make tricky decisions. Not because they wanted random chance to tell them what to do, but because the outcome almost always gave some insight into what they really wanted to do. If the coin "told" them to make Decision A and they found themselves feeling disappointed, they took this emotion as a sign that they unconsciously were already expecting Decision B!

Luckily for us, we don't have to employ such dark arts to gain more mastery and awareness over our own unconscious mental processes.

The cognitive appraisal theory also speaks to your *perception* of how well a situation meets your goals and expectations, so your emotions will reflect that. This theory says that it's our evaluation of events that causes us to feel certain ways about them. So, we feel positive emotions for an event that we have appraised as having some kind of benefit for us, and negative ones when we perceive some kind of threat or drawback.

Understanding this theory means that you can better evaluate your emotions by always determining what thoughts accompany them and how these interpretations and analyses actually line up with reality . . . or not. For example, you walk into a room, and a crowd of people bursts out laughing. You feel embarrassed because your appraisal of the situation goes a little something like this: "They were laughing at me." What caused this emotion? Not the strangers laughing, but your *thoughts about the meaning behind this action.*

This way of looking at things is keystone in what's called cognitive behavioral therapy (CBT), and in many ways, it may seem overly simplistic. Nevertheless, the above theory is useful for background about other, more-involved theories of emotion. If you simply pause and become aware of two things:

1. What are my expectations here?
2. What are my interpretations and appraisals of events?

then you might find yourself at a very good starting point for better understanding yourself and your emotions. It might help you realize if you are holding subconscious expectations one way or another.

The second explanation of the nature of emotions is that they are purely an interpretation of the body's signals.

Psychologists William James and Carl Lange proposed that emotions are just the perceptions of change in the physiology of your body—for example, changes in heart rate, breathing, perspiration, and hormone levels. This theory argues that emotions such as happiness are merely a physiological perception instead of a judgment as the previous theory states. Other emotions like sadness and anger are also mental reactions to different kinds of biological functions.

According to James and Lange, your body's state will change first as a reaction to an external stimulus, which will spur you to associate an emotion with it. For example, imagine you are about to perform a speech in front of a group of people and think of your body's reaction beforehand. You might feel your heart pumping faster or your breathing increasing slightly. Your mind will associate the combination of these physical reactions with a feeling of nervousness.

There is undoubtedly a connection between emotions and physiological changes. However, the problem with this account is that bodily states are not nearly as fine-tuned or diverse as the many different kinds of emotions. Returning to the previous example, your heart pumping and increased breathing may also be interpreted as a feeling of excitement because of the close physiological similarities—and this is where you may start to wonder whether personal interpretation and appraisal might come into play. This is the problem with associating emotions with physical reactions, because you often have more emotions than reactions, and many biological responses are too similar to differentiate.

Some theorists claim that the basic physiological reactions to environmental stimuli are a little like primary colors. Just as you can create a whole rainbow of different shades with just red, blue, and yellow, by mixing and increasing or decreasing the intensity of different "primary emotions," you can create some of the subtler, more complex emotions. Boredom, for example, may simply be a very, very mild form of disgust.

Understanding that emotions may be tied to your physical reactions also means you may be able to convince yourself of alternative emotions. Imagine you are about to partake in some public speaking. Telling yourself that you are excited instead of nervous, considering the similarity in bodily reactions, may help you better face the task ahead of you. It can be quite beneficial to perceive negative physiological signs and use them for positive purposes.

Neither of these theories tell the entire story; one is focused on emotions as thoughts, and the other is focused on emotions as physiology. In truth, they work hand in hand.

Emotions, in the most general definition, are neural impulses that move you to act. They are something the brain commands to achieve a better existence, one that has evolved over time to help us survive and meet certain needs.

Psychologist Linda Davidoff defines emotion as a feeling that is expressed through physiological functions such as facial expressions, heartbeat, and certain behavior such as aggression, crying, or covering the face with hands. According to her, emotions are a result of changes in the brain, where neurochemicals such as dopamine, noradrenaline, and serotonin increase or lower the brain's activity level according to what is more beneficial in the circumstances.

For example, the human emotion of love is proposed to have evolved from circuits in the brain that were stimulated and designed for the care, feeding, and grooming of offspring. Having offspring around eventually cemented these pathways and associated it with positive nurturing behavior. Oxytocin is released primarily during childbirth, breastfeeding, and cuddling, but as the theory goes, this bedrock emotion has evolved over time to our social and cognitive understanding of love. Gives a new meaning to calling your loved one "baby," right?

Emotion makes us act a certain way based on the stimuli that we have processed and is the interpretation of a series of physical changes. When you are in a situation where your palms begin to sweat, your heartbeat increases, and you are actively searching your surroundings, your body will do these physical things without much thought. They are reactive. But your mind will subsequently interpret the combination of these behavioral changes with a feeling of fear. First you have the stimuli, then the physical reactions, and then the psychological reaction—the emotion—that comes after.

It's important to note that often the brain is wrong, and the brain's concept of "beneficial" is not always compatible with the modern age.

When neurologists deeply explored the brain, they discovered that depression, love, kindness, aggression, abstract thinking, judgment, patience, instincts, and memories all have specific biochemical causes and even physical locations. Because all of these feelings, emotions, and characteristics have foundations in the brain, this means that they can all be radically affected by brain damage and brain surgery.

One of the most famous examples of brain structure altering emotions and personality is the curious case of Phineas Gage. In 1848, a work explosion led to a metal pole going straight through Gage's skull. Despite the injury, he survived, albeit with an enormous hole in his skull and with a sizable part of his brain missing for the rest of his life. The damage to his frontal lobes caused a radical change in his personality and character. Prior to the accident, he was conscientious, upright, and respected. After the accident, he was suddenly abusive, profane, irritable, and irresponsible. He was simply a different person, unrecognizable to family and friends.

There was no other possible conclusion other than the areas that were destroyed regulated certain parts of the personality and certain emotions. Later, neurologists explained this more precisely, in that the brain's frontal lobes are associated with moderating impulsive behavior, setting goals, and other abstract areas of thought. Those around Gage described him as having become fitful, irreverent, prone to the "grossest profanity which was not previously his custom," and "a child in his intellectual capacity" but with "the animal passions of a strong man."

Gage's case was one of the first true revelations that proved that emotions originated from a biological source and were a direct result of the brain, instead of being associated with the soul, heart, or simple expectations. This is important since it strongly suggests that our appraisals and cognitive evaluations of things are not the source of emotions—or more accurately, they're not the *only* source.

Modern research indicates that during events, the sensory information that you pick up is transmitted to the thalamus, the relay center of the brain, before being transferred to the amygdala and the prefrontal cortex. The amygdala instantly processes the information and sends signals so that hormones are released that activate the autonomic nervous system. Meanwhile, the prefrontal cortex slowly processes the sensory information from the thalamus in the background, a slower system overall.

The amygdala causes a person's instantaneous response to an emotion-evoking event. There is no thought in this; it is pure instinct. The brain has evolved to have two different tracks of stimuli-processing: one quick and one slower. The quicker one is designed for protection and survival: when the amygdala thinks there is a threat that must be acted upon immediately in one way or another. Alternatively, the prefrontal cortex is responsible for gradual processing, which allows someone to evaluate the emotion-evoking event and even regulate their emotions surrounding it—and this often happens long after the immediate stimulus is gone.

This fast and slow reaction can be seen in everyday life and is much simpler when seen firsthand. If there is a sound in the middle of the night that wakes you, you will instantly be alert and ready for action, even if you've had little sleep and your whole body is exhausted. This is an instinctual reaction to a threat so that you have a chance at survival. This is something that can easily be traced back as a result of evolution. If you are slow to respond to threats, you will not be able to survive.

On the other hand, the slow processing of external stimuli in the prefrontal cortex is for less-instinctual emotions. Something like love takes longer to process because of the number of contributing factors. It is not instinctual to feel love when presented with an event or situation. It takes a bit longer and more processing of the overall situation.

So what are emotions? We've discovered that they are part biological and part based on evaluating the world around us. But they are far more than that, as any romantic comedy will show you. Perhaps the best and most helpful way to conceive of emotions is this: They depend on your unique brain chemistry, your circumstances and status quo, your expectations, and your entire life of experiences that inform everything prior.

The Purpose of Emotions

The purpose of emotions really stems from that track of processing that goes directly to the amygdala for instant action. Emotions evolved for a reason.

They are one of the most important indicators of what will keep us alive and happy by letting us know what we should avoid and what we should pursue. Think of emotions as the mental version of your sense of taste. You will avoid foods that don't taste good, such as rotten fruit, because they are likely to be bad for you, and you will actively eat what tastes good to you because they are likely to be good for your health and survival—though not your waistline. Of course, this is why fat tastes amazing and why feces has a foul smell. Consider that for flies and other insects, feces must smell like heaven! Why? For them, it represents a precious and nourishing location that supports the survival of their eggs and larvae. So, they've evolved to pursue, not avoid, that smell.

Emotions go a level further than helping you avoid rotten fruit (or go for it, if you're a fly . . .). They help you avoid dangerous situations, psychological damage, and less-subtle dangers that are just as fatal.

Emotions lead to the well-being and ultimate survival of both individuals and groups by providing a quick and automated reaction to certain events and circumstances. This is so that we can avoid danger and take advantage of opportunities. This can be seen in both animals and humans. However, unlike animals, human emotions often clash with socially and culturally acquired conventions and rules. In this case, these automated responses may actually be disruptive and less adaptive than consciously deliberated responses. Tears of sadness may garner sympathy, but it can also denote weakness and a moment when someone's defenses are down.

Emotion is beneficial because it causes an organism to carry out certain preset behaviors that have been adapted over time to lead to the best outcome. In most cases of emotion, our movements lead to developing an intense focus on the object that triggered the emotion, something that focuses all our attention. This can be seen in behaviors like freezing in place, fleeing from a threat, or nurturing our young. All these actions are caused directly because of our reactions to specific emotions. If it's not positive focus, it's negative, paranoid fixation. They both assist survival.

An example of this is when a herd of deer is grazing, and even if only one of them hears the slightest noise, the entire herd looks up and concentrates very specifically on its surroundings and is able to identify and focus on a nearby lion before fleeing. A human example might be when a parent hears their child scream from across a room. They are immediately focused on nothing but their child and develop tunnel vision until they find out what's wrong. This happens because we are inclined to have a much greater focus on the object that causes whatever emotion we are feeling.

Along with pure survival instinct, emotions also serve to alert us to threats based on our past experiences. We all develop "emotional programs" that we adopt in situations that warrant emotion. For example, we have had to learn how and whom we can trust, how to cope with failure, and how to react to death. These all come with behaviors that we have had to learn over time so that we know how to act in certain emotional situations.

Based on the above, the purpose of emotions is to first detect evolutionary survival cues, then trigger reactions that have worked in the past and that we have deemed as good solutions to those problems. It is a continuous commentary on how we, and others around us, see the meaning of things. Some emotions are automatically signaled because we have such an immediate and quick reaction to them. Other emotions, such as jealousy or guilt, can be harder to identify and consciously react to. In either case, emotions help us because we are able to see what they are pointing an arrow at.

You may have noticed that since emotion has the convenient purpose of keeping us alive, it tends to have a negative bias. Negative emotions are more noticeable to us because attending to negative events is often more important to our survival than dealing with positive events. The worst outcome when you delay a reaction to a positive event—for example, a birthday, a promotion, or a wedding—is that you celebrate a little later than you normally would have. However, with a negative event, there are much worse things that can happen if our reactions are delayed. It seems quite appropriate that we focus on dealing with negative things first, as they have the power to kill us, whereas positive events merely enhance our well-being.

There is an infinite number of ways that situations can take a turn for the worse rather than taking a turn for the better. The night before a big event, we are most often thinking about every single thing that could go wrong, not everything that could go right. If any of these possibilities actually occur, you need to deal with them, so it's better that you imagine them and aren't caught off guard. Appropriately, negative emotions take up more mental bandwidth. Avoiding death is simply more important than eating cake.

There is no shame in feeling your emotions; we simply want to do so in an appropriate and healthy manner.

In a 2012 study, psychotherapist Eric L. Garland of Florida State University gathered fifty-eight adults in treatment for alcohol dependence and measured their responses to stress based on heart rate when exposing them to alcohol-related cues. The results found that those who restrained their thinking and suppressed their emotions more had much stronger stress responses to the cues than those who suppressed less frequently.

Even if you think you have successfully bypassed a stressor, there is no guarantee that your subconscious has also stopped dwelling on it. In 2011, psychologist Richard A. Bryant of the University of New South Wales in Sydney conducted a study where half the participants were told to suppress an unwanted thought prior to sleep. Those who tried to suppress their thoughts reported that they dreamed about it more, a phenomenon called *dream rebound*.

Both of these studies demonstrate that emotional suppression not only doesn't work but can also be immensely harmful. It can cause you to fixate more on what you are avoiding and can be detrimental to your physical health. As if this wasn't evidence enough, another study in the United States by experts at the Harvard School of Public Health and the University of Rochester showed that those who fail to say or express how they feel increase their risk of premature death from all causes by about thirty-five percent. When researchers evaluated specific causes of death, they uncovered that the risks increased by forty-seven percent for heart disease and seventy percent for cancer. Death rates are highest among those most likely to bottle up their emotion rather than express it to others and let them know how they feel.

All of this is to say that no, mastering our emotions does not mean that we suppress or deny them. Rather, it means that we learn to understand them so that we can consciously choose our actions instead of allowing ourselves to be pushed around by forces we don't see or even understand.

Emotions are at the center of almost all that we do and who we are. They add color and dimension and meaning to life, and existence would be pretty meaningless without them. And yet we don't have to be held hostage by them. We must strike a fine balance between fully feeling them, not suppressing them, and regulating them.

Takeaways:

- Our emotions have enormous power over us. Sometimes this is good, and other times, it makes us feel completely out of control. This is bad. But there is good reason for this type of power—you can view emotions as a type of warning signal that has evolved alongside humans to keep us alive and healthy. In the absence of higher critical thinking, emotions taught us about the world and how to regard it. This is also the reason that negative

emotions can make us spiral out of control so quickly.
- These types of dangers aren't present anymore in our modern lives, and our task now is less survival and more controlling and harnessing our emotions. The extent to which we do this can wholly determine how our lives go. In no way is this suggesting that emotional suppression is the key to happiness. In fact, emotional suppression is linked to poor health outcomes, so we must simply find the fine line of healthy emotional expression and reaction.

Chapter 2. The Keys to Eliminating Emotional Triggers

Emily is having a brilliant day out with her family. They're at a theme park for the day; the sun is shining, and she's in an excited, carefree mood. Her mother asks them to pose, snaps a picture, and then shows Emily the photo. "Cool, looks great," says Emily, but in fact from that moment, her mood starts on a steady downward spiral, and in an hour, she's feeling miserable.

We've all heard it and we've all felt it: a small provocation that can send our emotions spiraling in a direction that we didn't anticipate and that objectively shouldn't have any impact whatsoever.

This could be that one song that reminds you of something extremely traumatic, or maybe that one person you don't see often enough, but when you do, your emotions are out of your control. It could even be mentioning a single word, such as a name or the word "fat" that is the tip of the iceberg in terms of what it represents to you. For Emily, the photo made her think a certain cascade of thoughts: She saw how old her father looked in the photo and realized all at once that this just may be the last time they get to come to this theme park as a family.

This sets her off thinking about the death of her grandfather the year before, and in no time—seconds, even—she's unhappily mulling over the idea of death itself and her own mortality, and she even finds herself wondering, "What's the point of it all if everyone you love will eventually disappear?"

These are *emotional triggers*: things that elicit an immediate emotional response. Like the trigger on a gun, it can be small and its movement slight, but the result of firing that emotional gun can be devastating. There are positive and negative triggers, but we don't need help with positive ones. Some can lead to positive emotions, like discovering an item from your childhood that you immediately associate with happiness or love. It boils down to something you have a special sensitivity to, and it can impact you for the entire day or even week. With only a few words, you are feeling entirely off-center and fall into a pit of anxiety, depression, guilt, or shame.

Why are we so deeply affected by something that we rationally know should not affect us as badly as it does? Can't we be logical creatures that aren't ruled by our emotions?

Yes and no. We have emotional triggers because we have lived, struggled, and come of age. Our triggers are proof of our experience. No matter how lucky you have been in life, you have had moments of hardship and trauma you never want to experience again. Things that happen in the past, especially when we were children, are often ingrained deep into our minds. We may not have been able to deal with the pain or suffering or embarrassment that we felt when we were younger, so we suppress it—in fact, that's the logical part.

We work hard to avoid, deny, or ignore things to keep our days pain- and worry-free. And years later, when we are adults, reminders of our pain can bring those feelings screaming back. It's not productive to go completely down the Sigmund Freud route and assume that all of your adult pains are the result of childhood traumas, but we can say that our triggers and causes of pain from which we want peace and escape are rooted somewhere in the past. For Emily, this trauma isn't some psychological complex bubbling up from memories of a deep dark childhood—it's the very real trauma of losing someone she loved just a year ago.

Within the past, there is usually a story accompanying our pain or trauma; sometimes it isn't something you can pinpoint, but a variety of events that lead to a painful idea overall. There is nothing wrong with you if a painful memory triggers pain; it just means you're human. It doesn't mean you're weak or mentally ill, because everyone does the same. It's just a feeling that we have because of what something may lead you to think or what something may represent to you.

For instance, the pain of being constantly berated and ridiculed for being overweight as a child is something you can easily imagine causing multiple emotional triggers in adulthood. You may be extremely sensitive about your weight, or you might have developed eating disorders to cope with those feelings of inadequacy. You might feel an overwhelming need to exercise for hours a day, or you might still have a terrible body image and see an obese person in the mirror.

After you are triggered, how do you act when you suddenly experience great pain? You retreat into whatever habits or defense mechanisms you've developed over the years. For some, this will be physically withdrawing, while for others, it means a complete mental breakdown into a state of hysteria. The worst reactions will prevent you from living your life as you want, and this is the real downside to feeling our emotions fully. For Emily, the cruel irony is that her negative thought processes actually cause her to stop enjoying the day out with her family, and even if this *were* her father's last day on earth, she was too upset and distracted to appreciate it.

The word *trigger* is an important point here. The idea of an emotional trigger is that it is something that occurs automatically. One of the goals of this book is to move away from this automatic, involuntary path and onto a more conscious path. A gun will always fire if you pull the trigger, but luckily for us, emotions are more malleable. "Between stimulus and response, there is a space," said Nazi concentration camp survivor and author Viktor Frankl. "In that space is our power to choose our response."

By learning how to identify your emotional triggers, you can start to seize control of your compulsions and respond rather than react blindly to them. Once you start becoming aware of these triggers, you can begin to monitor them and realize that you can intervene in the period of time between the trigger and your response. This intervention is the key to changing the outcome of the situation and trying to get a more desirable result.

Emotional triggers often lie behind some of our worst behaviors. If you think about negative behaviors that seem automatic or out of your control, then you may just be unaware of the emotional trigger that caused it. Have you ever found yourself saying "I'm sorry, I don't know why I did that"? Chances are, you were triggered and responded so automatically that your conscious mind was scarcely aware of what happened. In Emily's case, the thoughts may be so swift that she finds herself feeling miserable—but has *no idea why.*

Triggers are very personal. Different things trigger different people, and so a trigger for you may not affect another person at all. The emotional intensity that is felt by a trigger is of a similar intensity as the initial trauma itself, which perfectly explains why anyone would want to avoid it. These triggers can be activated by any of the five senses: sight, sound, smell, touch, and taste. A trigger can even be another thought or emotion, itself triggered by another stimulus. This explains why someone like Emily got caught up in a downward spiral. This is the old familiar pattern where you feel depressed about being sad, or ashamed about being embarrassed, and so on.

When looking to better respond to your triggers, you need to identify the trigger itself first. The external stimuli may appear to be innocent (because, in a real way, it is!), but it could be a trigger simply because of what it represents to you. It may have nothing to do with the words that someone said to you and more to do with the links you make in your mind.

Perhaps a comment is made about you never attending college. This is a plain fact, but it may also make you think about other things you never had the chance to do or things that you missed out on. It might make you feel small and inferior to the people around you. Does this comment mean that you are dumber than the people around you? Is everyone in on the joke except you? How dare they imply that traditional higher education is the only way to be a respectable member of society!

A single sentence has the power to unlock all of these wayward thoughts. Because it's a trigger, sometimes you can't help but follow this train of negativity. The following thoughts have nothing to do with the initial trigger, but you are led there regardless.

It is the *story* of the trigger that is important, no matter how significant. Finding the story behind the trigger is key to solving it and changing your responses.

The Nature of Triggers

For our purposes, we will think about triggers as purely external; there is an external event that gives rise to an internal reaction. External triggers might be benign or harmful by themselves, but remember, they aren't necessarily related to why you might experience an emotional breakdown. Examples of external triggers include the following:

- being rejected or abandoned
- helplessness in painful situations
- being ignored
- being misunderstood
- when someone is angry at you
- being mocked
- being treated unequally
- when someone doesn't make time for you
- being vulnerable or exposed
- when someone shows disapproval
- being blamed or shamed
- being judged
- when someone isn't happy to see you
- when someone is trying to control you

None of these are rare in everyday life. In fact, someone might not actually be rejecting you, but it's what you will perceive if it is a trigger for you. For some, they are just the tip of the emotional iceberg and are related to much deeper-rooted pains and wounds. This is why people's emotions may escalate very quickly in response to a trigger. In other words, the former list of triggers is a direct reminder of negative associations involving the following list:

- acceptance
- respect
- being understood
- being in control
- attention
- being needed or liked
- being treated fairly
- being included
- predictability
- safety
- insecurity
- pride
- lack of confidence
- love

There are repeated and overlapping themes. Once these emotions are triggered, the typical response is certainly not to calmly address it, but rather intellectualize it out of existence or lash out in an attempt to cope. Both tend to lead to self-destructive behavior, and this also means the next time you face the same emotional trigger, it may even have a worse effect on you.

The coping mechanisms that we develop as a result can vary. We may create interpersonal conflict, act in a passive or aggressive manner, or stop communicating at all. The problem with these negative coping mechanisms is that over time, they will become patterns that produce further emotional stress, drain our energy, and influence our lives and our work. You'll begin with distress about your trigger; then the distress will compound as you notice the effects of your negative coping mechanisms and how much you want to stop your behavior patterns. These self-destructive habits may include the following:

- lashing out at people
- becoming needy and attention-seeking
- becoming a people-pleaser and ignoring your own needs
- completely withdrawing from others
- deflecting blame onto others
- becoming addicted to soothing behavior, such as food, alcohol, sex, drugs, shopping, and so on

The whole situation, from trigger to coping mechanism, is doomed from the start because of all the negativity that surrounds it.

Imagine you are at work and are asked to do a certain task, such as handing in a report or something similar that your employer expects and trusts you to complete. You do as you're told, but his feedback is not ideal. Though you may have put a lot of time into the project, he is unsatisfied and finishes off by saying he is disappointed.

Those words could be the trigger for you: the idea of disappointment. It isn't so much that you have to fix the report—that's something that will only take an hour or two. It's the fact that you let someone down. Maybe you can relate that to your own childhood and a situation where your parents depended on you but in the end weren't able to rely on you after all. The weight of a parent's disapproval is hard to accept even as an adult, but especially as a child. Logically, you know you aren't a child any longer and the situation is different, but triggers aren't rational. Someone in a semi-paternal role to you, your supervisor, has given you a negative evaluation, and that brings feelings of inadequacy flooding back.

From there, you become withdrawn and turn away from everyone else, especially those who care about you. Being alone only allows the negativity to fester and build further, and you begin to wonder if people hate you. Negative thoughts sustain themselves by adding more negativity to the fire, and you will berate yourself even if you're not sure why you feel so badly. Subconsciously, the story you've told yourself from childhood is in full effect. Feelings of insecurity, anger, remorse, or guilt will make themselves felt as well. You are feeding into a constant cycle where every rejection or disappointment will lead you to replicate this behavior, and this compounds as you feel bad about the behavior itself. Is there even an exit for this ride, or are you doomed to stay in the cycle?

Does this sound familiar? You can easily recognize this as self-destructive behavior, but it's not so easy to stop the freight train when you're in the heat of the moment. This is a classic example of an external trigger (the disappointing comment from your supervisor) that digs deep into your psyche and conjures up something that is only tangentially related (the disappointment from your childhood). This isn't a sequence you can stop without deeper self-understanding.

Emotional *Needs*

Specifically, we must understand what emotional need is being exposed or poked when we encounter an external trigger. The trigger is like a sharp dagger digging into a soft spot of weakness in your psychological armor.

For example, a common emotional need is the need to be in control, which may have stemmed from not having control at an earlier stage of your life. These needs aren't bad; in fact, they have served you extremely well in the past. The reason you have them is because at some point in your life, they allowed you to reach a certain goal or enabled a certain outcome. Your life experiences may have taught you that success depends on maintaining control, creating a safe environment, and surrounding yourself with people who appreciate your organization.

So what might happen if you feel that someone is subtly trying to wrestle control away from you, even if all they say is, "Well, what about *this* restaurant instead?"? It might seem that your emotional need for control is being destroyed, and rather than deal with the discomfort of not having control, you make sure that you can keep it and that others know it. All of those options are unpleasant for everyone involved, especially when they occur loudly in a split second.

By the way, the list of emotional needs has a complete overlap with the list of negative associations from triggers:

- acceptance
- respect
- being understood
- being in control
- attention
- being needed or liked
- being treated fairly
- being included
- predictability
- safety
- insecurity
- pride
- lack of confidence
- love

Of course, the less these needs are fulfilled, the more your mind will actively search for situations or events that threaten them. Your mind becomes volatile, and you start to think only in terms of self-protection and security. Someone may try to simply assert their own opinion, and you may react negatively because you see them as trying to cause havoc in your life.

At this point, you need to judge the truth of the situation. Are you really losing the need that you have? Is something actually being threatened, or is your reaction borne solely out of vicious defense? Only you can answer that, but in most cases, your reactions and emotional responses are far more about you (and your stepped-on emotional needs) than anyone else. We'll talk more about how to handle feelings of discomfort and emotional distress in the next chapter, but for now, all you need to do is ask yourself "Why?"

You need to consciously acknowledge the need that is triggering your response or you will be enslaved to that need. If someone wants to try a new approach to an activity and asks you first, are you really giving up your control? Are you hanging on to a certain feeling rather than responding to the situation at hand? Can others indeed be trusted to take care of things and also not hurt you simultaneously? And for that matter, is the need for control as imperative to you as it once was? What will happen if you do not possess it at every moment of every day?

Understanding emotional triggers will have a very real impact on your life. You may not even realize that some of your negative habits are a result of triggers. If you find that you are following distinct patterns of emotional triggers and then have a reactive negative event, then it is time to do something about it. Own your emotional needs and understand that you are acting out of pain and longing—everything that occurs afterward is just a projection of this. There's no reason that dealing with reminders of your past should be so painful and destructive.

The Emotional Spectrum

To better understand our emotional needs, we actually need one additional foundational skill: being *accurate* with our emotions.

In doing so, we must define the entire emotional spectrum so you know what you are dealing with, can guess where it came from, and then can react in the most optimal way. A doctor is only effective if she can diagnose the underlying sickness. Once that is achieved, she can prescribe medicine and actions to help that particular sickness. We can't seek to strengthen our emotional resolve if we are taking a stab in the dark at what emotional needs are feeling depleted.

Emotional granularity is what we are truly seeking when we think about accurately expressing and feeling our emotions. This is the process of understanding what you are feeling by putting a specific name on it. It seems insignificant, but you will be able to release some of the intensity of the emotion just by labeling it.

This is because there is a certain amount of tension from uncertainty and a lack of clarity about your feelings. Consider when you visit the doctor and have an illness, and the diagnosis is elusive. This is uncomfortable because you feel an intense lack of control and knowledge. Contrast that with immediately receiving a diagnosis and, subsequently, a plan for treatment.

People who have finely tuned feelings and are very in touch with their emotions are said to exhibit emotional granularity. It's not about being able to complicatedly label every emotion you have or just expand your vocabulary so that you can do this. It is about experiencing the world, and thus yourself, more precisely. By doing this, you will be able to better identify what it is exactly that you're feeling, and by identifying it, you will be able to understand the reasoning behind it.

Emotional granularity was coined in the 1990s by Lisa Feldman Barrett, who asked hundreds of volunteers to track and monitor their emotional experiences for weeks or months. All the participants in the study used the same vocabulary to define their emotions with standard words such as "sad," "angry," and "afraid." However, the study found that some people used the words to refer to distinct and differing experiences. Each word represented multiple emotional concepts and feelings. Others in the study lumped these words together under a single conceptual meaning, basically alluding to the feelings of being miserable.

According to Barrett, the greater the granularity, the "more precisely" you can experience yourself and your world. This means that you can pinpoint how you feel and better identify a solution. By using different words for different emotions and individualizing your vocabulary, there are many more benefits to your emotional health. We become what we label ourselves, and this can either help or hurt you.

People who were able to learn diverse emotional concepts were able to understand more finely tailored emotions. Emotional granularity can have a large influence on your health and well-being because it equips your brain to handle a wider range of emotions that you may experience. In other words, by knowing what you're feeling, you know better what the causes and underlying emotional needs are, and you know how to solve it.

For example, you may be feeling a combination of sadness, boredom, restlessness, and yearning, and without the proper understanding of your emotions, you may just generalize it as feeling sad.

But this does not solve the problem because it may not be exactly what you're feeling. However, this all changes if you have emotional granularity and are able to correctly identify your emotion as loneliness. Lumping emotions together means that you may not know how to deal with them, but identifying them all as distinct, independent emotions promotes understanding. Acting to fix a general feeling of sadness is a far different course of action than acting to fix loneliness.

The better your understanding of what it is exactly that you're experiencing, the more flexibility your brain has in anticipating or prescribing actions. It is easy to generalize or dismiss what you are feeling, but it is much more effective to give it some thought and pinpoint exactly what your emotional state is.

One step to take in increasing your emotional vocabulary is to take a look at the true spectrum of emotions. Quick, try to name as many emotions as you can. How many did you come up with? Here, the spectrum is represented by Robert Plutchik's wheel of emotions (courtesy of wired.com):

The purpose of this wheel is to provide a visual method for identifying a variety of emotions and to help relate them all to each other. Emotions on the outside, such as love, are a combination of two emotions in the petals beside them, in this case, joy and trust. Similarly, awe is a combination of surprise and fear. In this way, you can view a range of different emotions and you can visually map which ones are similar and what emotions make up others. You may have been able to name only five emotions before seeing the wheel, but you can now see there are subtle differences and degrees for each. You can probably also imagine circumstances that would create each feeling and match the corresponding faces.

Understanding emotional diversity is fundamental to our well-being. A study led by Anthony Ong of Cornell University investigated the effect of emotion on health. The study suggested that happiness is too often considered the emotion most strongly connected to a healthier body. The researchers found that feeling a wide range of emotions—what they termed emotional diversity, or *emodiversity*—may be the link to better health. This includes negative emotions and is another powerful argument for understanding emotional granularity and familiarizing yourself with Plutchik's wheel.

Ong had participants keep a journal of their emotions for thirty days. The participants had to rate the extent to which they experienced sixteen positive emotions that day. Happiness, enthusiasm, determination, pride, inspiration, and strength were among the positive emotions. They also recorded any negative emotions they experienced, such as sadness, anger, shame, and guilt. Emodiversity was measured by the number of different emotions felt by a person, the overall distribution, and the number of times each emotion was felt.

Ong found that people who experienced a wider range of emotions, including negative ones, were better at regulating emotions, keeping their cool, and refraining from using alcohol as a coping mechanism. He explained by comparing the emotions to a natural ecosystem, which is healthier when each various species serves its specific, functional role. If any one species becomes too dominant, it destroys the balance of the entire ecosystem and causes, for example, the dodo bird to go extinct.

Emodiversity similarly helps us prioritize and regulate our behavior so that we can cope and adapt to any given situation. Experiencing many different but specific emotions has more adaptive value than experiencing fewer emotions or more general ones. This is because the more specific emotions provide richer and more useful information to guide our decisions and how we face challenges.

For example, if you identify that you are feeling a variety of emotions such as anger, shame, and sadness, this will be more useful to you than just saying you feel "bad," which is a general term that doesn't provide you with much insight into how to solve the problem.

By specifying anger, you can then delve into what or who made you angry. By specifying shame, you are implying that you yourself have done something that you may regret. By specifying sadness, you may believe that the cause of your current emotional state shouldn't have happened and you want to fix the issue. All these points of action simply come from being able to identify your real emotions. If you had just stopped at feeling "bad," you may not have done anything at all. Indulging in the full range of negative emotions simply prepares you.

Admitting you have emotional triggers and needs is only the first step to emotional resilience and calm. This chapter takes the additional steps of understanding emotional granularity and the overall importance of attaching a name to feelings. Indulge in your emotions and feel the entire spectrum of possibilities. Your happiness depends on it.

Takeaways:

- When we talk about emotional resilience and calm, we are really talking about the emotional triggers that push us over the edge. The vast majority of the time, these triggers will be subtle and external and not at all proportionate (or even related) to the response they will create within you. This is the classic case of overreacting to a simple statement based on how it made you feel, not the actual substance.
- Of course, this is because our emotional needs are being exposed, poked, or prodded in an uncomfortable way. To escape this discomfort, we react by lashing out,

avoiding, or coping in a variety of other ways. Very few of these habits are healthy, and this sequence of events is what will lead to your unraveling and emotional instability.
- It's not enough to simply know your emotional needs; we need to gain emotional granularity into what is actually happening. A doctor can only treat a sickness if they know the actual cause, and Plutchik's wheel of emotions is a useful tool in labeling yourself and escaping the uncertainty of a general feeling of dread and discomfort. In fact, diversity of emotion helps us remain balanced and even-keeled.

Chapter 3. Recognize, Respond to, and Regulate the Chaos in Your Brain

Alex is at his girlfriend's house when she steps out for a moment, and he notices her phone ping. He can't help but see the message that flashes on the screen. He doesn't read it, but he notices the long string of pink heart emojis it ends in. His girlfriend comes back into the room, and he scowls at her. Within the next five minutes, Alex's reaction can only be described as a meltdown. He yells out in anger, makes vicious accusations, and then leaves in a ferocious tantrum, announcing that the relationship is over.

That's scenario 1. Scenario 2 starts the same way but ends completely differently. Alex sees the message and instantly notices his knee-jerk reaction. He feels a powerful flood of emotions—anger, jealousy, hurt, fear, disgust—but he takes a deep breath and tries to think. *Aware* that he is having this response (i.e., not completely flooded with the response), he decides to talk to his girlfriend the moment she comes in. He raises it with her calmly and neutrally. The girlfriend checks her phone and laughs. "It's my sister! She's telling me about this casserole she made. Here, look, she sent a photo. What can I say? She loves food more than she loves me!"

Our emotions are not always reliable. Recall that they are geared toward ensuring the survival of our species, but that's a goal with somewhat lesser priority in modern daily life. And even if, unlike Alex above, we are correct in our appraisal and our emotions are "right," it still doesn't mean that we need to submit to them and have them run our lives. Had Alex instead discovered his worst fear, for example, it would still be in his best interest to keep his cool and stay in control.

We already know that suppressing emotions is not the answer and that you should allow yourself to feel even your darkest of feelings so that you can release them. But there is a time and a place for indulging in all of the emotional needs we have discussed, and sometimes you may just not be in the right situation to do so. So, while you are entitled to *feel* angry and even vengeful, it's not a good idea to actually *express* that emotion—especially if expressing it would mean getting out of your car and strangling the person who's just stolen your parking spot!

Regulating your emotions means dealing with your emotional needs in a healthy and socially acceptable way. This chapter will explain how you can release your emotions in ways that

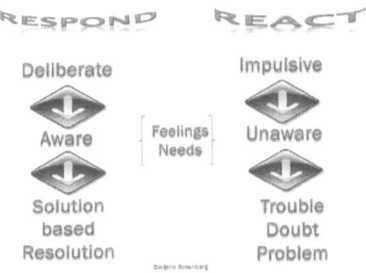

won't make you embark on a downward spiral.

Emotions are a constant part of our lives. Every minute of every day, we will feel something, and our emotions can change in an instant. There are highs and lows that you experience every day, and how you deal with them can significantly affect your mental state and well-being. Your ability to regulate the vast number of emotions that you feel also affects how the people in your life perceive you. When you are caught up in these moments, it can be difficult to regulate your emotions and think of the consequences, but the more you do it, the more it becomes habitual.

The first and foremost way of thinking about emotional resilience and calm is the *react versus response* model. It is succinctly summed up in the image below:

Overall, emotional regulation begins and ends with this image. To *react* to a situation means a complete lack of regulation because there is no thought. It is impulsive, short-term thinking. If we touch a hot stove, we react by yanking our hand away as quickly as possible to avoid a burn. All we are focused on is immediate relief, and rational thought is not possible during this phase.

To *respond* is to take time to consider the alternatives and make a decision based on the information you have. It may not always be the right one, but you won't be acting on impulse or elevated emotions. This is where rational thought lives, and either healthy coping mechanisms can be utilized or the emotions are given time to process and freeze over. It isn't just about controlling what you feel, but also about thinking rationally about what the best course of action is. It is the "gap" between stimulus and response that Frankl talks about. To choose our own response, we need to actually be aware of that gap and know how to take advantage of it. Focus less on your intense emotional impulses and more on desired outcomes and rational decisions. By doing so, the gap becomes bigger.

This is obviously impossible in the case of the hot stove, but it's very, very rare that we are encountering the emotional equivalent of a hot stove (perhaps the prospect of someone in a fit of road rage coming after you and your parking space!). The problem is that we continually view any transgression as something that requires an immediate reaction, and this becomes hardcoded into our habits until we are a walking volcanic reaction (and not response). Thus, the important part to recognize here is that you are probably so used to reacting that this chain of events cannot be mentally separated for you.

But here's something important to remember: *You don't have to react at all.*

Just because you have an emotion, and just because you've been triggered, it doesn't mean you are compelled to act. Nobody is forcing you.

Well, except habit—but conditioned responses, if we become aware of them, can be changed.

When you wake up in the morning, you use the bathroom, brush your teeth, wash your face, and put your clothes on. Is it likely that you'll forget any of these elements? No—because just like your emotional reactions, they cannot be mentally separated from the trigger. They are linked in a way that is so natural now that you cannot imagine any other way.

Now let's imagine an example of a fight between a couple about where to spend the holidays. In this situation, it may have been that you both wanted to spend the holidays with your own family and that they wanted you to spend it with theirs. A *reaction* to this might mean that you immediately discount the other person's opinions and assume that they want to control your actions or that your family doesn't matter. Without even thinking about the purpose and weight behind your partner's words, you simply begin to throw blame, feel anger, and then pick a fight about priorities. (Of course, there are some emotional needs being exposed here.)

Responding would be entirely different. The first step of responding is to take a moment to think and ask *why*. The answer may be that they haven't seen their family in a far longer time. What if they have a family member who is in ill health? What if they dislike your family, as your mother always lobs passive-aggressive statements about their weight? This brief pause of consideration allows you to understand the other person's perspective and allows a rational discussion where both people will be satisfied or, at the very least, a conclusion will be reached.

When you ask why, you also start to take a closer look at your own reaction. You realize that you are not responding to some absolute objective picture of reality but are merely expressing your own needs, seeing through your own perspective, and trying to meet your own needs.

And moreover, you may not even be doing this in a very effective way!

Responding is almost never *easy*, but it is *simple*.

Differentiating between reacting and responding is the first step toward true emotional regulation and keeping even-keeled. It's the first place where self-awareness can be your best friend.

A Regulation Framework

After one or two instances where you've chosen the path of responding versus reacting, you may begin to see the value of keeping your emotions in check. It's one of the most difficult tasks in the world, especially if you don't have much practice with it. This is the first and arguably toughest step, and there isn't much I can tell you about it other than to breathe deeply, make sure not to act when your heart rate is elevated, insert as much time as possible between the external trigger and your response, and continue to ask yourself on a constant basis, "Why am I feeling this?"

Soon, you'll require a new set of tools for greater emotional control. This is where a framework for emotional *regulation* comes in handy. You'll find that you are responding versus reacting, and yet your emotional state may not be upbeat or happy. You are still annoyed and peeved, even though you haven't acted out. And even if you *do* choose ultimately to act out in the way your impulsive self would have first suggested, this is in fact a completely different action because you chose it. It was deliberate and conscious. You were driving it, and not your emotions.

Of course, some emotional responses require no regulation—mostly positive ones. Laughing at a friend's joke or crying during a sad film are acceptable behaviors in their specific contexts. If an emotion is appropriate and helps you feel better, then there is no need to regulate.

But consider a different example: your impatience and anger at waiting in a long line. It might make you feel better (might!), but expressing your irritation and annoyance is neither appropriate nor productive. In fact, it might make your life significantly worse if you annoy others, and they're less likely to want to help or comply with requests.

But then you might be wondering, "Sure, I can work hard to restrain my irritation, but I still feel irritated! What am I supposed to do with that emotion?" How can you regulate something like this by either expressing this frustration in alternative means or regaining your emotional composure? Stanford psychologist J. J. Gross came up with a five-step method for regulating emotion.

The first step is to select the situation.

It's a question of prevention. This means that you should seek to avoid situations that trigger unwanted emotions in the first place whenever possible. If you have an allergy to peanuts, you can simply stay away from them. If you turn into a rage-monster when having to wait in line, find a way to go when there will be no line, or get someone else to go for you.

Imagine that you have recently decided to partake in a marathon. You've been training hard, eating healthily, and increasing your endurance. However, maybe you find that you lose motivation when you see others at the gym and they seem to be running so much faster than you or lifting so much more than you. You notice yourself feeling less and less inclined to go to the gym, and start feeling doubtful of your own abilities.

This is a perfect situation in which you can employ this step. Maybe instead you choose to go for more runs outside instead of in the gym. You avoid the situation that causes the feelings of self-doubt.

It doesn't mean that you are escaping your

problems or denying how you feel. It simply means that to keep your motivation up, you chose not to surround yourself with things that might bring you negativity. Of course, if you had been avoiding the uncomfortable truth about your own poor health choices and felt bad every time you walked past the gym on your way home from work, you might want to think about the best response. You could choose an alternative route and simply not think about how out of shape you are. But in this case, avoiding a triggering situation is not exactly healthy, and what's worse, it's likely to be ineffective in the long run.

Sometimes the best way to regulate a negative emotion is to never give yourself the chance to experience it in the first place. Remove yourself from triggering situations so you don't have to regulate at all. You have more of a say than you think!

The next step is to modify the situation.

This is when you cannot employ step one. Let's say that you work late and choose not to run outside because it's cold and dark. You know that at the gym, you normally have feelings of inadequacy and you wish to reduce this. This is where you have to *face* the situation you have been trying to avoid, so you need to modify it to reduce its impact on you. In other words, go to the gym, but change what you can about the experience.

You modify the situation to insulate your emotions by actively changing the terms for success. You alter your expectations to something that is more realistic and doesn't set you up for failure. Perhaps you go to the gym but you find a quiet, comfortable corner somewhere you don't have to continually watch others doing better than you. Maybe you go to the gym but during off-peak times.

Or maybe you modify *yourself* in the situation. You tell yourself that just because you can't go as fast as someone doesn't mean you can't run for as long, or that you can't improve with time. If you adjust the rules and make it so you are competing only with yourself, then you are in a can't-lose situation. You look at the other people there and don't feel threatened—after all, they are "running a different race!" You are the one writing the rules for yourself—why do you need to be so strict and harsh?

The third step is to shift your focus.

When you can't avoid or modify a situation, you can always change what you focus your attention on. If you're upset by something, you fixate on it to your own detriment. Instead of being preoccupied by runners who are faster than you, shift your focus to the gym-goers who are much, much slower than you. You can also shift your focus to yourself and your own running—perhaps you aren't running so fast because you're always distracted and discouraged. Concentrate on improving yourself and reaching your own goals instead of beating someone else. Or watch TV.

You don't need to compete with anyone but yourself. Whatever negative thoughts seem to be taking your attention, switch to positive ones. See the brighter side and try to feel gratitude for what you still have and others don't. It's quite difficult to feel both gratitude and emotional turmoil simultaneously.

Step four is to change your thoughts.

At the core of our deepest emotions are the beliefs that drive them. By knowing this, you can change your emotions by changing the beliefs that sustain them. Your negative belief is that everyone at the gym is judging you for your failures—therefore, your emotions will reflect that. Remember the cognitive appraisal model of emotions?

This is where you need to change your thoughts. To do this, think about how you view others at the gym. Think about the meaning you assign to neutral events. Most of the time, you don't really care what they do, or you think their performance is better than yours. By that reasoning, what if they feel the same about you? Believe that people don't judge and aren't even paying attention to you, and your emotions will follow and relax.

What is the evidence that your beliefs are true, and what is the evidence that they are not? If it helps, literally make a list and tally up the score. You may find that your negative emotion is a response to something that simply doesn't exist.

The fifth and final step of emotion regulation, when all else fails, is to change your response.

This is pure regulation. This is the last resort when no other steps of this process work and you find yourself feeling without limits. Maybe you do go to the gym, and you fully experience all the emotions that triggers for you. Maybe you feel utterly destroyed, decide to give up, and are very close to tears or rage. Here is the point at which you most need to rein in your automatic response.

Take a deep breath to gather yourself, close your eyes, and pause. Acknowledge the emotion, feel it, stare at it head-on, but *surf* it like a wave rather than letting it crash into you. Gather your inner reserve and force yourself at least to change your facial expression and *choose not to act.*

Obviously, you won't be able to all the time. I did mention that emotional suppression is unhealthy, but this is different because you are trying to make it to the point where you can respond instead of react. When we can reflect a bit more, often we will find perspective and a different and healthier way to respond. Your goal, then, is not to magically solve any problems in that moment, or strong-arm yourself into feeling differently. Your goal is only to ride out the emotion for long enough that you are in response mode and not react mode. By pausing in your tracks and taking a few moments to fully experience all your emotions, you will find that you can more actively regulate them.

You might have noticed something: The earlier in the process that you step in and act, the easier it is. It's not hard to avoid exposing yourself to triggers, but it's very hard, sometimes impossible, to rein in a negative emotional spiral once it's well underway. So, the logic is clear: As much as you possibly can, try to intervene sooner rather than later. Then, you don't need force and willpower, but only a little planning and foresight.

Another similar model is called the STOPP Method, created by Carol Vivyan. STOPP stands for:

- stop
    - simply pause and try not to let yourself be overcome by emotion
- take a breath
    - breathe deeply to keep your heart rate in check and notice your breathing in a conscious effort to keep it slow and measured
- observe
    - ask what is going through your mind, determine where your focus lies, discover what you are reacting to, and try to name the feelings that are swirling through your brain
- pull back for perspective
    - ask yourself what is really happening, try to incorporate different perspectives, understand how little it ultimately matters in your life, and remember to not instantly see disaster
- practice what works
    - proceed with the best action you can take for the time being, remember your values, make sure you are responding rather than reacting, and focus on your main goals for the situation at hand

Remember that inserting a delay between our intense emotions and our responses is always the end goal.

None of the steps in these emotional regulation frameworks are easy. And at some point, simply increasing your tolerance to emotional discomfort and anxiety becomes a necessary step toward resilience and calm. The more you can take, the less you need to regulate. You'll recognize some common elements from the regulation framework we've just discussed.

Distress Tolerance

Distress is a natural part of life. Every person at some point or another needs to face discomfort and anxiety; it's not a question of whether you'll have to endure it, but *when*. Fortunately, emotional resilience is something that can be learned and cultivated with a plan and frequent practice.

While many might choose to focus on avoiding emotional discomfort or arranging a life where they don't have to experience it, a truly resilient person trusts in their own ability to withstand distress and not just survive but thrive. Most importantly, having a higher degree of distress tolerance makes you hardier; you won't even have to use coping or self-awareness tools as often because you simply won't reach those heightened negative emotions as frequently. Greater tolerance to distress and anxiety can be mastered over time using just a few simple steps.

Step 1: Identify your triggers

It always goes back to the triggers, doesn't it? Whether this is a particular situation, an event, a person, words, memories, thoughts, body sensations, sounds, or images, a trigger is like a bell that starts us off down the path of distress. Sometimes, a pattern of distress can happen swiftly and without our conscious awareness, leaving us clueless as to why we're suddenly upset. One moment you're feeling fine and going about your day, and the next you feel the escalating sense of panic, anger, or sadness. But what happened?

If you look closely, you can always identify the precise stimulus that caused your emotional response. It's tempting to think that emotional control and mastery are all about wrestling emotions once they're already in full swing. But with practice, you can start to see the small seeds of distress *before* they sprout into overwhelming emotion that's hard to get a grip on.

Imagine a woman heads home for the Christmas holidays to be with her family. She starts the visit feeling calm and balanced and has told herself that she'll keep her cool even though her family is notorious for heated arguments and upsets during the holidays. Despite feeling okay for a while, she soon notices her mother's messy kitchen and feels herself getting agitated at how chaotic the food preparation is, with everyone talking over each other and weighing in on how best to prepare the Christmas meal. Then she notices she's starting to feel a bit physically warm, given that the fire is crackling away in the next room and several people in warm jumpers are bustling in and out of the kitchen. Finally, her father makes a hurtful comment about the way she is chopping onions, and like a dam breaking, she suddenly feels extremely angry and upset and snaps at everyone. In other words, she's distressed.

Rewind the situation and it's clear that there are several triggers instigating these feelings of anger and unhappiness. These are both external (noise and bustle, untidiness, criticism from loved ones) and internal (the feeling of chaos and stress, feeling too warm, not feeling good enough, or perhaps recalling negative memories and associations from childhood).

Triggers can be literally anything. Anniversaries, money problems, arguing with your family or spouse, workplace conflict, going to the doctor, taking an exam, falling ill, having to compete with others, thinking about the future, being rejected ... The list goes on and on.

How do you find out what your *own* triggers are? A good way to think about this is to look at past behavior and try to understand what's reliably caused distress for you before. This takes a degree of awareness in the moment, but can you notice any patterns in what occurs immediately before you become emotionally overwhelmed?

The great thing about becoming aware of your triggers is that when they occur, they give you an opportunity to stop and take notice of what is happening. This gives you the option to step in and take action before becoming overwhelmed with strong emotions.

Step 2: Pay attention to your warning signs

Of course, a trigger is just a trigger—it's our response to it that makes all the difference. A warning sign can be thought of as any indication that you are having trouble dealing with some emotional distress. Again, these can be thoughts, emotions, or the urge to behave in a particular way. They indicate that distress is underway and that you are dealing with strong unpleasant emotions.

What could happen at this point is that you resort to "escape methods" to try to avoid the distress. These kinds of behaviors can be as varied as the triggers that they're designed to avoid. They can include seeking assurance, distracting yourself, resorting to substances or overeating, oversleeping, or simply avoiding the stressful situation completely.

In the example of the woman above, the mounting emotional stress she experiences leads to a very clear warning sign: snapping at the people in the kitchen with her. Whereas the triggers might have been small bells, warning signs are more like blaring fire alarms. Warning signs are not just actions, however. They can be thoughts (for example, "I can't do this" or "I'm a failure") or feelings (for example, irritation, panic, depression, shame, or jealousy) or even physical body sensations (for example, fatigue, shaking, a knot in the stomach, tension, or tearfulness).

It can be difficult to clearly see distress as it unfolds in the moment, precisely because distress is so unpleasant and we're often seeking ways to avoid it at all costs. That's why the regular practice of distress tolerance will sharpen your ability to zoom in on your unique triggers and exactly how they affect you.

Step 3: Forego your escape mechanism and do the opposite

Step 3 is where your distress tolerance plan really comes to life. Being triggered and experiencing overwhelming emotional, mental, and physical sensations can force us down the path of automatic habits designed to make us feel better. However, *escape behaviors* seldom give us the opportunity to develop resilience and grow as people, and frequently the escape behaviors themselves are harmful to us.

For the woman in our example, snapping at family members is only likely to put them on edge and in turn feed the chaos and stress in the kitchen, unintentionally making matters worse. Other escape behaviors can be even more damaging—for example, binge-eating, alcohol abuse, or avoiding doing tasks at work that will only become worse with procrastination.

Though escape behaviors feel irresistible in the moment, and they may sincerely feel like our only solution at times, they are not ultimately adaptive and come from a place of avoidance, weakness, denial, and escape rather than confidence and strength to deal with what life throws our way.

How do you know what your escape behaviors are? This part of the process might be the easiest to identify since they'll be those actions you feel strongly compelled to do when in the thick of an overwhelming emotional reaction. Many people get intense cravings for sweet things after an upsetting argument or feel compelled to get up and leave the room if the situation feels utterly hopeless and overpowering. Look closely at those behaviors you feel unable to resist when emotionally overwhelmed and you'll likely learn something about your escape patterns.

The trick is then to deliberately and consciously commit to doing the opposite of that behavior, which invariably means to seek calm, not escape, and remain in the situation and emotion.

Triggers and warning signs are invitations to become aware in the moment and make the (admittedly difficult!) choice to take a different path. Luckily, this gets easier and easier the more you practice it. You might, for example, choose to quietly tell yourself, "I will stay with my feelings right now instead of trying to avoid them." You can silently say this sentence to yourself again and again in your mind, say it out loud, write it out in a journal, or even share your sentiment with someone close. The point is to bring your actions out into the open and convert old automatic habit into conscious action that you have a choice in.

Knowing what your triggers and warning signs are ahead of time can help immensely with this. If you know that you are prone to thinking thoughts like "this is unbearable" and resorting to self-harm to distract yourself, you may choose to instead recite a little mantra to yourself: "I *can* bear this. I am choosing to stay with my feelings and not escape them."

Step 4: Accept your distress and discomfort

Once you have identified your triggers and warning signs, and once you have made the commitment to stay present with whatever emotional responses emerge in you, the only thing left to do is follow through with it. Of course, this can seem easier said than done!

This part of the process can feel counterintuitive and, by its very nature, can be emotionally overwhelming. But again, frequent practice along with a willingness to stay with what emerges will eventually help you develop a tolerance for unpleasant emotions.

First, in order to accept an emotion, you need to be able to correctly recognize that it is occurring. Take some time to be still with that sensation, whatever it is. Try not to rush in to deny or avoid it, and remember that there's no need to embrace it, either, or pretend it isn't there. Simply give yourself and the emotion space to expand, and watch. What can you feel in your body? What sort of thoughts are in your mind? How do those thoughts make you feel? Why is this happening to you?

This exercise can be done during a more formal meditation, or you can simply choose to pause and take a moment out of your daily life to gather yourself and become aware of your emotions.

Next, try to gain some distance from the emotion by using imagery. It's so easy to get "swallowed up" by an emotion, feeling as though it is us and that we are completely identified with it. But emotions are temporary and passing. Can you find a way to let the emotion be what it is without getting carried away with it?

For example, our example woman may imagine that all the chatter and chaos and negative emotion of the family holidays is like a dark cloud of tangled words that she can wrap up in a beautiful pink balloon, where, once inside, it goes silent and peaceful. She can then stand outside of these emotions and hold them on a string, apart from herself. Another person might imagine that their sadness and overwhelming depression is really a small, tired person who just wants to sit at the table for a little while. By sitting across from this person and allowing them to speak, without getting upset about their existence, we can start to gain some distance and detachment. This is the beginning of emotional mastery.

As you engage with your emotions, whatever they are and in whatever image you have given them, pay close attention to your breath. Being focused on the simple inhale and exhale of your breath can ground you in the moment and remind you to stay anchored in the present. Wait out your emotional spike and see what is on the other side.

Part of the practice of learning to tolerate emotional distress is understanding that it is a practice (i.e., not something you master all at once and never have to look at again). If you are aware and accepting of the fact that you *will* experience emotional comebacks, you can remain calm when they occur and appreciate them for what they are: an opportunity to try again to turn away from avoidance and escape behavior and reaffirm your commitment to yourself.

Emotional strength and the ability to calmly withstand even the most unpleasant emotions is like a muscle: The more you exercise it, the stronger it gets. So be grateful for every opportunity you have to exercise it. If you feel strong emotions arising again, watch yourself closely. Are you frustrated with yourself for not "doing it right"? Are you impatient with the process, feeling like you should have succeeded with it sooner? Great! Take these feelings themselves and feed them back into your practice. Remind yourself of your commitment to doing the opposite of your escape behaviors. Remind yourself that you can and will stay with feelings and that all feelings, no matter how unpleasant, will pass. Sit with them and observe that, past an initial period of high stress and anxiety, they aren't overwhelming experiences—merely uncomfortable.

Step 5: Making friends with distress

We are all individuals, and nobody is going to experience distress in quite the same way. The only way to truly understand your own emotional patterns and behaviors is to get in there directly and become aware of them.

These five steps can be thought of as a closed sequence that improves and refines itself every time you go through a cycle. Every time you are able to successfully soothe yourself without avoidance/escape behaviors, take note and remember how you did it. Next time you are in a similar position, you can pull these activities, thoughts, or ideas out of your emotional inventory and use them. In essence, you are building greater awareness of yourself and slowly removing the behavior from the realm of passive, reactionary, and unconscious into the realm of deliberate conscious action that really serves you.

This final step is about taking stock of what works. This can be actively making a list of behaviors that you want to practice or simply taking a moment to quietly acknowledge progress when it happens. Make a note of words of encouragement, mantras, or images that help you get into the state of mind you're trying to achieve. Write them down somewhere you can easily access, or maybe try carrying a small object that encourages you to stay mindful.

In fact, once you begin to feel more in control, you can start to actively seek out exposure to distress in order to gain practice and strengthen your resilience. Though this may seem scary, in a way, it gives you more control to engineer situations that from the outset have you feeling prepared and confident.

If you'd like to do this, start with your triggers and think of a situation that may make you feel distressed. Of course, it may backfire to throw you in the deep end of distress—instead, think of an ultimate goal that you'd like to achieve and then set up a few gradual steps and smaller goals you can achieve to reach that. This "exposure ladder" is a series of manageable steps that increase in increments. Each step might involve spending more and more time in the distressing situation, or it may entail increasing the intensity of a sensation or an interaction with a triggering person.

As an example, a man might have trouble with watching certain highly charged news shows or movies as a trigger and resorts to overeating as an escape behavior. He commits to telling himself that he can, in fact, tolerate the feelings of depression and hopelessness this brings up. He sets himself a goal: to be able to watch a full news program without overeating to soothe himself. He starts with smaller steps. First, he watches five minutes. Then he watches two five-minute segments with a break. Then he watches ten uninterrupted minutes. And so on.

Whether you choose to practice an emotional exposure ladder or simply want to do your action plan when distress naturally rears its head, if you can stay with the emotion in the present, breathe, reorient your behavior, and reward any successes, you essentially train yourself toward greater emotional control and stability.

Takeaways:

- Now that we've got an understanding of emotional triggers, needs, pain, and how they all interact with each other, we must talk about how to deal with them. How can we inject self-awareness into our lives, recognize what's happening, and keep the volcano (us) from erupting? The first model to think about is responding versus reacting. When we touch a hot stove, we react without thought, instinctually, and protect ourselves. This is rarely necessary from an emotional standpoint, and yet we find ourselves similarly volatile to a volcano instead of pausing a beat to think and then respond.

- Next, we should think about a framework for regulation that plays with the emotional triggers and needs we have discussed. This consists of selecting the situation (avoiding triggers), modifying the situation (decreasing triggers), shifting focus (ignoring triggers), changing thoughts (changing the trigger), and changing response (reacting less to a trigger).
- This leads directly to the next point of distress tolerance. Sometimes we are indeed too prone to flying off the handle; we are overly sensitive in a way that makes us unpredictable and fragile. Thus, we need to work on increasing our tolerance to distress and anxiety. This has common elements with the framework for regulation, but it focuses more on foregoing the comforting escape mechanisms you use and staying in the situation and emotion. The purpose is to accept anxiety and distress, withstand the

major emotional spike surrounding it, and stay with it until it subsides and you realize that you are still doing fine.

Chapter 4. Figuring Out and Replacing Your Emotional Patterns

So far, we've talked about the purpose of emotions, common triggers and the emotional needs that underlie them, and some ways to respond and regulate in healthier ways.

These all constitute important knowledge about your inner workings, but at some level, they are just Band-Aids that we can apply over the emotional pain or discomfort you feel. The true cure to emotional haphazardness is self-awareness and understanding the origins of your emotions. It isn't just about why you feel a certain way, but also about how that feeling took root in the first place. Only when you understand the entire sequence of events, from outside (trigger) to inside (emotional need) to outside again (coping mechanism) can you hope to cut the cycle short.

In the examples we've looked at so far, there has been a pretty distinct and clear-cut episode or event that we can draw a box around. But try to imagine that the behavior of any one of these hypothetical people is actually a part of a broader *pattern*. It may seem obvious what the problem is and how to fix it when looking at these fictional stories from the outside in, but when it comes to your own life, things all of a sudden seem much, much murkier.

That's only because we are unconscious and behaving habitually. Unconscious, habitual behavior can be, for all intents and purposes, invisible. We do something because, well, we've always done it. There is no *why*. In fact, you could argue that if you do something often enough, it starts to be indistinguishable from your personality or character.

But it isn't! If you've ever felt like your own behavior was a mystery to you, or you struggled to imagine how else you could possibly behave, then that's a good sign that you could use more awareness.

Sometimes we find ourselves falling into a loop where we are simply in an autopilot state of acting and thinking, which will always lead to undesirable outcomes. Your feelings get hurt, you shout and react, and you compound your negative feelings with guilt and shame. You might think you are engaging in the framework of emotional regulation, and you might think that you are responding rather than reacting. But how can you know?

These automated actions are very difficult to see in the heat of the moment because we are so used to doing them without thinking. This is why building self-awareness and understanding the patterns of your thought and behavior are essential for emotional resilience. Without this, you will only be able to address the symptoms and not the cause.

There are a few tools for this, and they emulate talk therapy in some ways because they force you to really analyze your actions and answer questions that you'd rather not. You'll recognize a few elements of these tools from prior chapters, but there is always a different perspective in each new tool that can assist with self-awareness. Think of yourself as developing an inventory of different tools or lenses through which to view your own situation.

The ABC Loop

If you went to the doctor and told her that you were breaking out in hives, she would look you over and probably try to find the cause. Are you allergic to something? She'd maybe suggest you avoid a suspected food or substance, then watch to see what happened. In other words, to better understand the rash she sees in front of her, she needs to understand everything *around* that rash, i.e., what came before and what comes after. It's not that different from your behavior more generally. We can understand why a behavior exists if we can see what happens around that behavior.

The ABC Loop is a classic behavioral therapy technique that considers all the elements that contribute to a behavior. It stands for antecedent (A), behavior (B), and consequence (C). The middle section, the behavior, is often called the behavior of interest, and the technique works by looking at the before and after to understand why the behavior in the middle occurred. It's also what you want to examine and regulate or control—hence the increased scrutiny on it. In isolating these three elements, we can begin to understand what is actually happening in the external world and how it relates to the emotions we feel.

Let's begin with the antecedent. This is the environment, the events, or the circumstances preceding the behavior of interest. Anything that happens before the event that may contribute to the behavior would fall into this category. If you're wondering whether antecedents are like triggers, then yes, they are! An antecedent, however, can be almost anything, and it isn't necessarily conscious.

When identifying the antecedents, consider where and when they are occurring, during what activity, with whom they occurred, and what any others were doing at the time. Write down a mental snapshot of everything you can recall; you never know what might be pertinent to the ABC Loop.

For example, perhaps you are someone who finds yourself constantly arguing with your parents. You might realize that most of the time, you don't even agree with what you're arguing with, but you do it anyway. You want to stop this behavior, so you think about the last time it occurred. Set the scene first. In this situation—dinner at your parents' house, early afternoon—things were going fine, the television was playing, the topic of the future came up, and you were talking about your job and your career goals. This is the antecedent.

In this case, it may be a certain word, phrase, or sentence, or it may be the ideas and feelings that come with them. It could be the time of day or even the time of year (did I mention it's Christmas, that special time of year when some of us rehearse some of our worst family feuds?). It may simply be the presence of your mom and dad, or the same living room that you've had so many difficult conversations in before as a teenager. You can probably see the value of growing awareness—the more fine-tuned your understanding of all these smaller causes, the more accurately you can pinpoint what actually triggered the behavior.

Then we move on to the behavior, which is the focus of this technique. This behavior can be either pivotal, which leads to further undesirable behaviors, or distracting, which can interfere with your own life or the lives of others. In this case, the behavior is uncontrollable anger, which is pivotal because it causes stress and irrationality in other parts of your life, too. It is important to describe the behavior in full when looking back in hindsight. There is some overreaction on your part, a complete lack of listening and validation on their part, and the feeling that you must make yourself heard. In this situation, there are raised voices, dramatic gestures, insults thrown, and intentionally vicious comments being said, most of which were irrelevant to the actual argument.

Now, when you're doing this kind of "behavioral postmortem," it's important not to get bogged down in irrelevant details. It doesn't really matter who was right or wrong in this disagreement, or what precisely was said or not said and by whom. Rather, try to zoom out and look for broader patterns and for how one emotional and behavioral state is flowing into another.

Last is the consequence of the behavior. This outcome is important because it often reinforces the behavior. If the consequence is genuinely undesirable, most unwanted behaviors will not be repeated, but if there is some sort of reward that is incidentally received, then the behavior will continue.

In this case, the outcome may be that one of your parents, usually your mother, leaves the room upset and the dinner is cut short, whereby you then go home. However, you might feel that you have "won" the encounter by making your mother back down, and this would be a positive reinforcement to continue engaging in this sort of behavior. But is it actually positive if everyone has been worked up to a frenzy and is feeling the adrenal residue of a loud argument? You got a little piece of satisfaction, but it's probably not a net positive interaction here.

The next time you're over for dinner, there will be an awkwardness hanging in the air. After all, the disagreement wasn't resolved or moved forward by anyone's behavior, so it's likely to repeat. This time, though, everyone has already had some warm-up and the argument can kick off with even more intensity than last time!

So what do you do once you've identified these three parts? Now comes the analysis. The antecedent, as mentioned before, is the family dinner. It is important to mention the last thing to happen before the behavior. In this case, it was questions about career goals and aspirations. Already we have identified an important factor of the situation. Considering this is the last casual question before the argument, it is clear that this is the catalyst. If you are looking back at your own event and are able to identify the catalyst, consider why it affects you so much. Do you always react in the same way? What about in other similar situations—can you see any patterns?

If you can identify what it is that catalyzes a behavior you want to stop, then you can focus on it and actively try to redirect your behavior when you encounter a similar situation again. This is where we also start to think about emotional triggers and needs. Why is this so triggering for you, and what need is it uncovering that isn't fulfilled? This doesn't happen with everyone, just your parents; why are they triggering you, and what emotional need is intensified with them specifically?

The next thing to observe is the behavior itself. In this case, it is uncontrollable yelling, but it can be a whole range of different ones. Think about why it is that you choose this behavior. In this case, maybe you feel as if you're not being heard. Maybe you want to exercise some control or authority or overcompensate because you are feeling cornered. Whatever the reasoning behind it, think about what purpose it serves. Usually, this is a coping or defense mechanism. But is it actually helping? Your purpose here is actually to make sure that your emotional need is either defended or fulfilled—is your behavior working toward that goal?

If not, is there another way to behave to get a better outcome with regard to your emotions? Even if it is something as simple as taking a moment to calm down, leaving the situation, or telling someone that you are not in an emotional state to continue, find a way to redirect your behavior so that you produce a different emotional outcome.

The last thing to consider is the consequence. If it is a recurring behavior, then that must mean you get some reward out of it. In this scenario, your mother has left the scene directly after the argument and you are forced to go home. Maybe this is exactly what you want—to spend less time with your parents. Maybe you just want them to support your career, and when it seems they aren't, then you don't wish to be there anymore. Maybe you want to score a "win" over them or be the last person standing and have the last word.

Have you learned anything from this experience, or is the consequence simply that you will double down on your behaviors from before? Do you feel compelled to change anything to make it so that your antecedent isn't triggered even worse next time and the behavior doesn't keep growing in proportion? An easy question to ask is the following: Does the consequence make you feel good or bad?

One important thing to keep in mind as you're working through this process is not to concern yourself with blame or shame. You are only seeking to understand yourself better, so take on an attitude of respectful, neutral curiosity, rather than one where you are trying to pounce on perceived flaws or find ways to point the finger at others for "causing" your unwanted behaviors.

Consider the overall outcome of this event that we have analyzed with the ABC Loop. We can see that we are emotionally triggered by some combination of our parents and the topic of the future and that there is a particular emotional need or pain that comes out in this setting (antecedent). Next, we see that our behaviors are a somewhat unhealthy response to this emotional need and pain and aren't necessarily about the topic or setting by themselves (behavior). Finally, we observe that we've defended our emotional need and pain so hard that we cause turmoil in the relationship (consequence), and though this is a small victory for your emotional shields, it only makes the antecedent and behavior more likely to be amplified in the future.

How can you change this sequence of events to make sure it doesn't happen again in the future? It always starts with questioning yourself and asking why you feel such emotional pain—this is what leads to the behavior and then to the consequence, where the cycle repeats all over again. You can cut off the conversation before the emotional pain reaches a boiling point, or you can make sure that the behavior is something that soothes you and helps you cope.

For instance, if all you want is to be supported in your decisions, have a conversation that deals with this and leave it when it doesn't. If there is something you don't want to discuss, tell your parents that there are things you would prefer to be off-limits and you might discuss when you're ready; leave it if they keep pushing you.

The ABC Loop helps you understand how to cut the cycle of lack of emotional control, and it explains why things tend to get worse over time, not better. It gives you the exact blueprint for better emotional resilience and calm: Avoid or alter situations that can turn into an antecedent, and attempt to choose healthier behaviors when you are triggered.

Emotional Dashboarding

Emotional dashboarding is a similar process to the ABC Loop. It also encourages stepping back from a situation to review your actions and reactions to break your autopilot. While the introspective approach of emotional dashboarding is the same as the ABC Loop, there are a couple more incremental steps:

SITUATION/ FACTS	THOUGHTS	EMOTIONS	BODILY SENSATIONS	IMPULSES/ ACTIONS
Example: Project due tomorrow	*"I don't feel like doing this." "I shouldn't have to."*	*Sadness, boredom, irritation*	*Heaviness, fatigue*	*Go to sleep, eat, space out*

Situation. Jot down the literal facts of the situation—details that couldn't be argued by any observer. This means leaving out opinions and existing prejudice or bias. This will help you understand the circumstances around your bad moods or emotional outbursts.

- A project is due tomorrow.
- Your spouse's family is arriving for the holidays.
- You're assigned a new supervisor.
- You've moved to a new place after a breakup and are invited to a party.

Thoughts. Recall the personal interpretations and thoughts that went through your mind when the first feelings of distress or avoidance came up. These are the beliefs and thoughts that are triggered by external events. Often, these are far more volatile and violent than the following examples because they lead directly to the next step of emotions and emotional needs and pain. Really try to articulate your inner monologue, as it can literally tell you everything you need to know about your mental and emotional state.

- "I don't feel like doing this." "I shouldn't have to."
- "Last year they seemed judgmental about the appearance of our house."
- "I've heard bad things about this person from people who've worked under him."
- "I'm not sure I'm ready to mingle with strangers in an unfamiliar place."

Emotions. Take a measure of the feelings you experienced during this conflict using only single emotion words. For our purposes, be sure to also think about the emotional need or pain that is being invoked. Make the connection from the external actions to your thoughts and to your emotions. See them as a continual cycle, a cycle that we are trying to understand and ultimately cut in favor of something healthier or happier.

- sadness, boredom, irritation
- resentment, disfavor, annoyance
- anxiety, fear, concern
- dejection, tension, uneasiness

When naming your reactions, ask yourself three times why these emotions came up. The repetition of the question will encourage you to go as deep as possible and get to the root of the problem. In the first example, what mental picture caused the sadness about the late project—fear that it won't be good enough? Is the boredom because you feel it's a routine that keeps recurring? Are you irritated because there was a social event you would rather have done tonight?

Look at the second example—you feel resentment when you imagine that your in-laws are judging your home.

Why do you feel resentment?

Because they are judgmental and it doesn't feel fair to be judged that way.

Why do you feel it's not fair?

Because we work just as hard as they do, but they think that we're somehow inferior to them when we're not.

Why?

Because we made different choices in our careers and had different priorities. But they don't see that or understand the values we're living by.

You could even continue asking *why* to get a deeper understanding of how your thoughts, feelings, and behaviors are connecting. Can you tell that just by asking why repeatedly, you are already uncovering some additional nuances to how you feel? This may simply mean reframing the way you're seeing the problem. For example, you might have originally said that their presence was to blame for your feelings, but after exploring those feelings, you discover that there is also a certain insecurity in your own lifestyle choices, or perhaps a realization that you don't feel seen or heard as the unique person you are by your extended family.

Bodily sensations. Mark down the physical sensations you felt when experiencing the conflict. These can add clarity to your emotions because while we can lie to ourselves, our bodies can only react and will almost always tell the truth.

- heaviness, fatigue
- stomach upset, headache
- shoulder tension, increased heartbeat
- lightness in head, slight tremors in hands

Be as literal as possible in describing bodily sensations. Avoid metaphors like "my heart was jumping out of my chest"—instead, say, "I felt my heartbeat accelerating." Sometimes our bodies know something far sooner than our brains can register. There's a reason so many of our metaphors and idioms have to do with the body!

Impulses/actions. Write down your first instincts of what you wanted to do to relieve or avoid the conflict—things that made you feel good, distracted you, or minimized your attention to the preceding sensations. If these are relatively benign or healthy, that's a good thing. However, if your first impulses are to react with rage or lash out at someone, then you know a chord has been struck. Something is happening within you, and it is being demonstrated through your actions.

- go to sleep, eat, space out
- watch TV, surf online
- do "busy" work, make phone calls, scream a little bit
- drink alcohol, walk outside

Like the ABC Loop, the practice of emotional dashboarding produces a sequence of events that can be broken down and assessed like a fictional story. Why did this happen, how can we prevent it, and what elements seem to be your downfall? The dashboard adds a few internal elements—internal conflicts and physical sensations—that play the same role that "motivation" serves in fiction. Recognizing those alterations in your feelings and thoughts can help you identify them when they come up again.

Another great thing about slowing down and separating out the components of your experience this way is that you empower yourself to intervene in different ways. Sit down with a diary and literally tease apart a situation (especially a recurring situation) and experiment with what you'd have to rearrange or change to produce different results. Many people assume that cognitive behavioral therapy is the gold-standard for this kind of work, but the truth is that you are never fully able to change any thoughts, feelings, or behaviors until you *actually know what those are*.

Don't assume that just because a thought, behavior, sensation, perception, idea, or feeling is automatic that it is fully under your control, or that you completely understand why it is there and where it is coming from. Remember that these reactions often occur from force of habit alone—not because they make sense or because they're getting us the results we want.

One method may seem more appropriate than the other, depending on your circumstances. You may want to use the ABC Loop when initially coming across a conflict, then the dashboard if it happens again or gets worse. If you sense your spouse's family being passive-aggressive or judgmental at your house for the first time, you may choose to run an ABC Loop first. If it happens again in another situation, you might want to run through the dashboard to see if you can gather additional insight about your moods and reactions.

It may simply be easier or more efficient just to execute an ABC Loop. Or perhaps your discomfort is so acute that you'd rather run the emotional dashboard. With honest self-inquiry, either method can help you make headway in discovering patterns and identifying troubling behaviors to change.

Three-Step Cognitive Behavioral Therapy

The very genesis of your emotional patterns comes right from the source – you and the way you speak to yourself. Even if something isn't objectively true, if you hear it 100 times, you might just start to believe it.

CBT is evidence-based and well-suited to tackling the inner dialogue that accompanies worry, anxiety, regret, shame, grief, guilt, blame and low self-esteem. Life is filled with challenges, adversities, and unexpected events. These can either be viewed as painful and unfair, or manageable and growth-inspiring—all depending on the mindset we cultivate with our self-talk.

CBT is not about "thinking positively" but thinking more clearly, realistically, and neutrally—without cognitive distortions. In CBT, our thoughts, feelings, and behavior are all interconnected, i.e. if we can change our thoughts, we can change our feelings and consequently how we act (and vice versa).

We've covered some cognitive distortions already—catastrophizing, black and white thinking, etc.—and have begun recognizing the language of negative self-talk in ourselves. Observing your thinking and becoming aware of previously automatic thoughts and distortions is step 1.

Step 2 is learning to gently and consistently challenge these thoughts and their underlying core beliefs, testing just how accurate they are. We considered this in the previous chapter where we asked ourselves questions, tested our assumptions, and encouraged ourselves to seek alternatives.

Step 3 is doing the work of replacing these distorted thoughts and beliefs with ones that are healthier, more accurate, and more likely to lead to a balanced and optimistic life. Before we move on to this very important step, however, we need to look a little closer at the language of negative self-talk, and how to spot triggers and warning signs so that we can step in and stop cognitive distortions *before* they take flight in our minds.

Step 1: Observe

Self-talk is made of words. That's all it is.

It's literally like a film script that you run internally. But words can be edited, deleted, rewritten. In previous sections, we've focused on fact vs. fiction, and the importance of comparing our thoughts against objective reality as much as possible. This is a way of fine-tuning the *content* of our thoughts, but there's also the question of the style, grammar, vocabulary and tone of the language we use when we talk to ourselves.

You've utterly failed, you big fat idiot.

You didn't pass the quiz that time.

Both of these statements can refer to the same event, and in a way are factually equivalent—i.e. "didn't pass" is the same as "failed." However, it's obvious that they carry very different emotional nuances, and will have very different effects on the person thinking them.

Automatic, negative self-talk has a certain flavor that you can recognize with practice. It's usually short, spontaneous and emotionally loaded with strong words, or has a rambling, looping quality. It's filled with overgeneralizing language like *always, never, nobody, should, nothing, must, completely*, or language filled with guilt, self-flagellation and judgment. But they truly can be tricky, and some are even disguised as positive. Observe the following.

"I just don't have the energy to get up early in the morning."

> This thought might seem harmless. Given a hectic day, this even seems justifiable. But is it? Think about it from what you have just learned about self-talk. You are instructing your brain to take any effort to wake up in the morning. In a way, you are weakening your brain's ability to adapt.

"I don't have enough time to update my resume."

> Sure, you are busy. This is a way of stopping yourself from doing the work that will help you get the life you want. Another way of weakening yourself from taking action.

"I can't remember names no matter how much I try."

> The number of people who believe this surprises me. Some even take pride in it. If you keep drilling time and again in your brain that you can't remember names, then what do you expect your brain to do? It just considers whatever you say as the result you want and then creates that for you.

"I just can't stop myself from eating dessert."

> If you slip once and you treat it like it is a behavior set in stone, all you are doing is strengthening the physical wiring in your brain to always reach out for dessert. Even when your life depends on it.

"I just can't seem to lose weight no matter how much I try."

> Of course you can't. First, stop eating that dessert, and even when you do occasionally treat yourself with a dessert,

stop instructing your brain to take no effort in getting that extra pound off you.

"I ought to control my spending" finishes as ". . . but I am unable to."

> This is just a way of torturing yourself with guilt. Take some time to reflect whenever you are tempted to say this. Usually, it is going to be after a purchase you've made that you know you shouldn't have. Think about what drove you to buy that item. What was the feeling evoked? Was it an impulsive buy? Did buying that item fulfill the intent you had in mind? Thinking things through will give you insight into the root cause of your behavior that you can then use to decide on the right self-talk that will help you get rid of the problem.

"I should try to get to work on time" ends with ". . . but I can't seem to."

> Life happens. Sometimes you are genuinely stuck in traffic you did not anticipate. Other times you aren't waking up early enough to be ready to leave for the office on time, hence the delay. Whatever the cause, the above statement does not help. It is just another form of level-one self-talk.

"I know I should study harder" ends with "... but I don't."

> Just reading it once seems overwhelming. Now think about telling yourself this time and again. The only thing this does is give your brain the impression that whatever effort you are putting in is not enough. This doesn't motivate your brain to study harder as you intend it to. Instead, it creates guilt for not doing enough, thus demotivating it from taking any action toward studying harder.

Watch for language that spirals or feeds on itself or steadily mounts in intensity. Look out for thoughts that you accept as true immediately in the moment without a second thought. Automatic thoughts are usually strongly infused with feelings of fear, anger or shame, and will appear in language that suggests this—at the very least, you'll know it's negative self-talk simply because you feel awful when you listen to it!

Step 2: Challenge

If you catch yourself in negative self-talk—congratulations. Even better, however, would be to avoid it altogether, or stop it before it happens using your knowledge of what usually triggers these thoughts for you. Negative thoughts are easier to recognize and handle when they are still small.

As a technique, "thought stopping" appeared in the late 1950s in the sport psychology world, and was used to cut short self-defeating and anxious thoughts that got in the way of performance. An excellent overview can be found in Zinsser, Bunker and Williams' 2010 book, *Cognitive Techniques for Building Confidence and Enhancing Performance*. The idea is to use a behavioral or mental cue to snap out of a negative self-talk spiral.

For those suffering from mental health issues like panic disorders, it can be especially hard to distract yourself once a negative thought appears in your mind. This technique acts as a tool to help become aware of and then replace these thoughts in a way similar to practicing mindfulness.

Pinching yourself, imagining a red light or saying "stop" out loud can all act as cues to bring your conscious awareness to the moment and away from negative self-talk.

It's essentially the art of beneficial distraction, and even more effective when you then quickly redirect your attention to a preferable subject (a more realistic thought, perhaps?) It's an assertive stance you are taking against that inner dialogue that you know only carries you to places you don't want to go.

The technique can potentially backfire if you end up constantly monitoring yourself to look for failures you can pounce on—the trick is to bring mindfulness to the process, not punishment or judgment. If you try this technique for a while and find it actually worsens the problem, ease up, be more compassionate, or simply attempt a different technique. Thought stopping may help for more superficial rumination, but not for deeper anxieties that may respond better to slow, deliberate engagement.

If you'd like to try the technique, however, here's how to begin:

Write down a list of all the most distressing, recurring, distracting and unwanted thoughts you wish to stop paying attention to. Try to rank them from most to least distressing. Include anything from "one day my boss is going to figure out how inept I am and fire me" to "this lump probably means cancer."

Next, do some prep work by practicing—sit alone in a private room and spend some time visualizing any situation in life where the most distressing thought might conceivably intrude. For a while, go into the thought and focus on it, feeling out its contours. Then, as abruptly as you can, stop the thought.

Stand up quickly, say "stop!" out loud, snap your eyes open, make a loud clapping noise or click your fingers. Empty your mind and try to hold that emptiness for thirty seconds or so. If the thought tries to intrude again, repeat "stop" as often as necessary.

What you are trying to do is gain practice at stopping rumination mid-thought. In time you can be less drastic with your interruption, and eventually internalize the "stop" so you only say it quietly to yourself. You don't necessarily need to use the word *stop*—you could also visualize your thoughts as traffic that stops dutifully at a red light. Try saying out loud "I'm having a thought about XYZ right now" to remind yourself that it's just a thought, and to gain distance.

Whatever you do, simply remind yourself that thoughts are just words—just a script that you can stop in its tracks and rewrite. The hard work is to recognize the thought, but once you do, realize it has no hold on you unless you pay attention to it. Make a habit of using certain phrases to interrupt unwanted thoughts, divert your attention and affirm your *choice* to follow certain thoughts and drop others:

Don't go there

Let it be

Let it go

It's in the past

Leave it alone

Focus

Don't pay attention

Slow down

This, too, will pass

It doesn't matter

Breathe

You've got this***

Using this thought stopping technique may make some people uncomfortable—aren't you just ignoring your problems?

It's worth remembering that thought stopping is best used for those thoughts that you know are intrusive, unwanted, and genuinely unhelpful. These are the thoughts that you have already identified as irrational, untrue, or exaggerated, and you know that entertaining them will only lead to stress and worry.

Your goal is to tolerate and manage anxiety, rather than turn a blind eye to it. Similarly, having thought stopping in your mental toolkit doesn't mean you are unable to hear your own intuition or engage when a situation warrants genuine concern. Thought stopping is merely a mental fuse that lets you halt catastrophic rumination before you get too carried away with it.

For some people, the thought-stopping technique outlined above may feel a little punitive and may not work for them. Thankfully, there are plenty of other techniques underpinned by the same principles. You could try scattered counting, for example. Counting to ten is a common anger management technique, but it's easy enough to become automatic, allowing your brain to carry on ruminating even as you count. Rather, jump around with random numbers to engage your thoughts more, e.g. "43, 12, 5, 88, 356, 90, 5..."

In the same way, a mantra or spoken word can interrupt runaway thoughts—choose a more complicated nonsense phrase or something in another language to prevent yourself from doing it too automatically. Alternatively, you can select affirmations based on your specific triggers or perceived negative qualities. Though they can take time to work, the reason so many find them effective is that our brains eventually come to think of them as true. These affirmations can be specific quotes from religious texts, or statements like "I believe in myself" and "I am in charge of my thoughts." These can be recited both mentally and out loud, but with conviction. Repeating lines you don't really believe will be pointless, so choose your affirmations wisely.

You could try self-soothing with encouraging positive self-talk, such as "don't worry, you can handle this" or "you're doing great!" Play a song you like or listen to a podcast to engage your auditory channels and pull attention away from anxious overthinking.

A distracting cue can also be physical in nature—physically move yourself into a different position, get up and do a few jumping jacks or go for a quick jog outside to break out of thought loops. You can also switch to more bodily/somatic awareness by simply focusing on your breath, and practicing a technique called muscle isolation.

Sit or lie comfortably, close your eyes, and then work your way through all your muscles, starting from the ones in your toes. Squeeze them as tightly as you can for five seconds and then release and relax completely. Then focus on the muscles in your feet and legs, moving up until you reach the muscles in your face and scalp. Not only will this help immensely to release physical tension, but it will distract your overactive mind and bring it more fully into the present moment.

Muscle isolation can be an excellent warmup to a more formal sitting meditation practice, or a great way to end a mindfulness session. Combine it with gentle soothing music or head outside where you can feel the sun and breeze on your skin.

Another classic CBT technique is to decide that instead of stopping or running away from scary and overwhelming thoughts, you'll simply stare them down and ask what's the worst that could happen. Look squarely at your ruminations and say, *so what?* It's rarely as bad as you think, and seldom something you truly cannot handle. Research has found that even those who lose their limbs or eyesight—suffering tragedies anyone would consider horrifying—soon return to a median level of happiness because of how powerful our modes of adaptation are. As such, no matter what it is you're worried over, you're very likely to be able to survive it just fine even if the event were to occur.

You might like to visualize yourself actually encountering the worst-case scenario with grace and poise, tackling the problem and seeing that it isn't in fact the end of the world, even if the worst does come to pass. This alone can take the steam out of your most catastrophic ruminations.

Step 3: Replace

Some thoughts are so useless and untrue that they can be discarded immediately, or stopped using any of the techniques described above. With practice, you'll be able to recognize totally harmful thoughts (like, "I'm probably going to die" or "everyone hates me") and release them immediately.

Some ideas and thoughts, however, are a little more subtle and are more appropriately rewritten rather than discarded entirely. These thoughts are often those that we believe have a grain of truth to them. Here, it's necessary to practice a degree of conscious discernment to determine what kind of life script will serve you best. Again, this is a step that can only be done *after* you've gained a good awareness of the kinds of self-talk you engage in—otherwise you risk having these techniques exacerbate rather than solve the problem.

For a quick example, say you want to eat healthy food but usually find yourself binging on desserts. I never eat unhealthy food. I no longer enjoy eating food that is not right for my health."You can do this silently or you do this out loud. Until now, if you had a pastry in front of you, you'd just start eating it without thinking much about it.

Say you are with your friends and everyone decides to order a pastry. Now when you cut a bite of pastry with your spoon, you say, "I no longer eat food that isn't right for me." First, your friends will look at you oddly, but you continue to say those words out loud and to yourself and for a while even keep eating the pastry.
.
After some time, when you have a pastry in front of you or any dessert, for that matter, your brain is automatically going to say, "If I never eat unhealthy food or food that isn't right for me, then why on earth do I have a plate full of dessert in front of me?"

It's about defining yourself in a different way, starting with your words.

Exercise 1: Think it through

This exercise takes some time and effort. The first step is to note down your self-talk using any of the methods already discussed (for example, by using a bullet journal, writing down your core beliefs or periodically taking a self-esteem inventory). Then, after a week, try to look for particular themes or patterns.

What kind of self-talk is it (for example catastrophizing or mindreading)?

What events, thoughts, feelings, people, or situations triggered the self-talk?

What common threads can you identify?

What was the effect or result of these thoughts?

What do they say about your core beliefs?

Reflect on what you see. Get some distance on your thoughts. This way, we're more likely to evaluate them truthfully, as opposed to in the moment when our feelings might cloud our judgement. Notice if your self-talk has actually held you back in life or made you feel bad. Ask yourself, how would it feel to have positive self-talk instead? What might your life look like and what could you achieve if you didn't limit yourself in this way?

In thinking through things carefully, the more positive alternative is likely to appear to you. For example, you may see that you constantly exaggerate physical symptoms and then get stuck in doom-and-gloom thought loops about what might happen if you fall ill. Seeing all this objectively noted on paper, seeing how it negatively impacts your life in many ways, and seeing how utterly irrational it is, you slowly begin to loosen the self-talk's hold on you.

By completing this exercise, you can begin to see the more accurate and realistic options available to you. Better yet, when you try them out and monitor yourself for a week, you may be surprised to learn just how much wasted mental energy and anguish you can avoid by consciously and deliberately dropping negative self-talk.

Exercise 2: Change channels

The previous exercise is a gentle way of supporting yourself as you naturally find your way to healthier cognitive alternatives. But you might need something a little more direct, especially for those core beliefs that are more persistent.

You can do this exercise alone or add it onto the Think it Through exercise above, and it's essentially what you would do with a CBT therapist. Write down a negative thought as it pops up. Now, deliberately reword the sentence in front of you until it is more neutral and objective.

- Remove all-or-nothing language like *never, everybody, none,* etc.

- Remove emotive and harsh language like *idiot, hate, fail, disgusting,* etc. Replace the word "difficult" or "impossible" with "challenging" and use "annoyed" instead of "angry." Use language that is more time-limited, for example "I'm feeling sad today" rather than "I'm sad," which implies a permanent state of affairs.
- Make the tone more neutral and compassionate.
- Instead of saying "can't" try saying "don't." Own your preferences and the place you're currently in. Rather than saying "I can't do it" simply say "I don't do it" or even "I don't want to do it." This doesn't shut off the possibility of doing it later; it's just a statement of fact, whereas "I can't" sets a hard limit.
- Similarly, avoid hedging language like "I'll try" or "maybe" or "I guess I could..." Speak directly and state what you'll do.
- Remove any outright falsehoods or attempts to mindread or predict the future.
- Phrase things gently and compassionately, as though you were speaking to a loved one or even a person in a professional context.
- You might like to add some positive phrases like the ones already covered earlier (e.g. *you've got this*).

- Remove assumptions and unsupported conclusions. You might try replacing these statements simply with "I don't have enough information yet," which is far more neutral and accurate.
- If you can, rephrase statements as questions. Instead of saying something is impossible, ask *how* it could be possible.
- Likewise, see if you can switch focus entirely and reframe things to the positive: instead of identifying limitations and problems, pinpoint resources, options, alternatives, and possibilities.
- Put the words in the mouth of a trusted mentor and loved one and see how they fit—what would they say instead? How would they phrase things?

Here are some examples:

Negative: "I embarrassed myself in front of all those people and they'll never ask me to do a presentation ever again."

Positive: "That didn't go as I planned but it's OK. I did my best and learnt a lot, and will prepare better for next time. It's not the end of the world if I receive some constructive feedback from my bosses."

Negative: "Who would want to have a relationship with an old, unattractive person like me? There's no point dating, nobody would look twice."

Positive: "I have no evidence that trying to meet someone new would be impossible. I deserve a loving relationship, so I'm going to put myself out there. Whatever happens, I can love and respect myself."

Negative: "It's hopeless starting a business in this economy, you'll only fail."

Positive: "I have faith in myself and a lot to offer. There are always options, and I'm going to do my best and keep a positive attitude."

After you've changed a statement, deliberately make an effort to redirect your attention toward this new version instead of more negative statements. You can combine this with thought stopping, halting the negative thought and then redirecting to your reworded script instead. Practice makes perfect, i.e. the more you tell your brain something, the more it believes it's true!

Exercise 3: Testing for accuracy

Some self-talk has been going on so long that it's become embedded in layer upon layer of assumptions, even becoming part of our identity and worldview. These beliefs take time to dismantle! Learning to get to the root of a statement's objective accuracy sounds easy, but it's definitely a skill that takes time and effort to master.

- Is your self-talk fact or opinion?
- Where does this idea really come from?
- What is the evidence and what assumptions have you made?
- Can you think of any counterexamples to disprove this idea?

Testing for accuracy can be as simple as noticing yourself say "nobody thinks my art is any good" and changing it to "I haven't shown many people my work, but I do remember that nice compliment I got once." Even the smallest positive that is demonstrably and objectively true can act as a counterweight to a whole universe of negative thinking that actually has no proof to support it at all.

Remember, you don't have to go to the other extreme—the goal of positive self-talk is not to become a narcissist who is incapable of accurately seeing their own faults. Rather, you are seeking moderation, balance, and a realistic and healthy viewpoint. You'll be surprised by how unremarkable "healthy" self-talk sounds in comparison to what you're used to!

You can use these re-scripting techniques in the moment you have a negative thought, or you can do it more systematically, for example at the end of a day when you sit down with a journal and reflect. You might include some mindfulness and guided meditation, too.

To commit to shifting to your more positive self-talk phrases, pin new phrases and affirmations to a wall or visible place. Start the morning by reading through them or regularly take five-minute breaks throughout the day to check in with yourself, breathe, and recalibrate, using these statements as cues.

All of these techniques can be used in combination. For example, someone might keep a self-talk diary for two weeks where they note down the thoughts that emerge as well as the triggers, results, and accompanying emotions that go with these thoughts.

They soon see a pattern: that much of their self-talk can be boiled down to the core belief "I'm not as good as everyone else" and that the low self-esteem behind this belief expresses itself in mindreading ruminations. For example, "They said they liked my shoes but I'm sure they think they're hideous and were just lying to make me feel better..."

Reflecting on this, the person decides that self-defeating attitudes like this one have only served to undermine them all through life, and that they are ready to embrace a more realistic, compassionate outlook toward themselves. They note down a range of thoughts that pop into their head throughout the day and then systematically ask whether they're all that true.

Is it *really* true that you are a failure? Maybe it's more accurate to say that you didn't do as well as you thought you would on one particular task, but that your overall performance is great. Is it *really* true that other people are sitting whispering amongst themselves about how awful you are? Far more likely is that people barely notice you and your missteps, because they are far too busy dealing with their own!

By gradually testing the truth of the self-talk we are increasingly aware of, we realize how many other options there are. We can try to rewrite some of the most commonly occurring thoughts and themes, with improved alternatives:

"They don't like me" turns into "They don't know me, but there's no reason for them not to like me."

"I'm falling behind in life" becomes "I'm doing the best I can and I'm on my own path. I don't have to compete with anyone."

"Everyone else is so much more talented compared to me" is reworded into "I admire the skills of others, but that doesn't mean I don't have good points of my own. Besides, I'm willing to learn."

These rewritten statements can be pulled out or recalled when the person spots themselves falling into a detrimental thinking spiral again. They can use the "stop" technique to halt negative self-talk in its tracks, then redirect. They can build in moments of meditation and self-reflection throughout the day, regularly using positive statements like, "you're just fine" and "don't go down that path" when negative self-talk rears its head. Here is one potential internal monologue:

"You're such a loser, you're doing all this stupid positive self-talk stuff and you know it'll never work, that's for other people, but you'll just mess it up. Besides, it's not negative self-talk, it's the truth—you really are a loser… STOP. Take a deep breath. Remember, these are just thoughts, not reality. I recognize this pattern. This is my inner critic and I've already decided I don't care what they say. You're doing great. Breathe. Now look at the situation again and make a conscious decision about your inner script. You're *not* a loser, you're working hard on your self-esteem and that's admirable. It will work with time. *It probably won't.* STOP. I already know what lies down that path, and I'm not biting. I'm going outside for a run…"

If the above stream of consciousness seems a little extreme to you, consider this: your mind is *always* running a script very much like the one above, but it may be conscious or unconscious. If it's unconscious, it will run along unawares, quietly affecting every aspect of your life. But if you can make it conscious, you can change it, and reap the benefits. It's your choice.

Though we've uncovered several different techniques and approaches to help you unravel unhelpful self-talk and gradually replace it with healthier core beliefs and supportive inner dialogue, the process is likely to be a lot more ad hoc in real life.

What's important is that your approach works for *you*. Try a few things and give them time to work, but don't be afraid of tweaking these methods to your own ends, combining them or trying something completely different.

Other helpful tips to keep in mind as you master the art of re-scripting your inner mental world:

- Do re-scripting work when you're calm and feeling optimistic, and not when you're stuck in the middle of a mental storm or feeling upset.
- Keep at it—it's better to do a little and often than expect that one session will solve everything forever!
- Run through your new script even if you don't quite believe it at first—with repetition, your brain will soon start to literally rewire itself.
- Don't be afraid to make changes to your script—you might not get it right the first time. Remember, it doesn't have to be over-the-top enthusiastic and

unrealistically positive. It just has to be neutral and relatively unbiased.

- It's up to you to evaluate your script as you go. How does the new self-talk feel? What effects does it have on your mood, your self-concept, and your behavior?
- Don't beat yourself up if occasionally you end up ranting, complaining or going down a stress rabbit hole—it's perfectly normal to be grumpy or pessimistic at times. Likewise, a little stress or criticism isn't the end of the world. Just keep things in perspective and try whenever possible to return to awareness of your thoughts *as thoughts*.

The language of positive self-talk flows naturally from a healthy self-concept. But if you're trying to undo the damage of a poor self-esteem, you may find yourself upgrading your negative self-talk in the hopes that it positively influences your self-concept.

There's no fixed script about what exactly to say when you talk to yourself, but speaking from the right frame of mind (i.e. from a position of self-respect and compassion) will get you most of the way. Nobody can tell you precisely the right words to use in your own mental dialogue. Your life context is unique, and every new situation will require you to respond spontaneously and authentically.

Using a pre-written script is a great first step—a little like mental training wheels as you find your confidence. But in time it should be easier to generate your own impromptu positive self-talk, in real time, and it will feel more and more genuine with practice. The end goal is not simply to rehearse a script, but to automatically and sincerely talk to yourself in a positive way.

Until that time, however, here's a brief self-talk checklist to make sure you're on the right track.

Positive self-talk should ideally be:

- Framed in present tense
- Simple and straightforward (statements that lead to endless cycles of rumination are likely to be negative self-talk whereas good, wholesome, affirmative self-talk is typically direct and uncomplicated)
- Honest, which means it must include potential room for improvement or shortcomings wherever relevant
- Personal and meaningful to you
- Able to make you feel better
- Practical and realistic
- Optimistic and hopeful—neutral is great, but if you're talking to yourself, why not be your own best friend and offer some

supportive and encouraging words while you're at it?

Takeaways:

- Our lowest emotional points don't exist in isolation; they almost all exist due to various cycles of triggers, emotional needs, behaviors, and then consequences—all of which strengthen the cycle for the future. So it's necessary to cut the cycle short and interrupt it in any way that we can. The most valuable way we can do this is through simply analyzing how it takes place in our lives.

- The first tool for this is the ABC Loop, which stands for antecedent, behavior, and consequence. They generally describe the main elements of an emotional outburst that we can break down and analyze: What happens before, what you did to cope, and what happens afterward that makes the cycle even harder to escape.

- The second tool is similar but more in-depth: emotional dashboarding. It describes the same cycle but through a different lens, with elements of situations, thoughts, emotions, bodily sensations, and impulses/actions. This gives you an even deeper view into certain situations and why you felt the need to lash out or become dragged down by negativity. The important thing to keep in mind with both of these tools is that the willingness for deep honesty is required.

- CBT is a popular and effective therapeutic framework that emphasizes our thoughts as the key component of our feelings and behavior. The underlying principle of its techniques is that our thoughts influence how we feel, which in turn determines the way we behave. This creates a feedback loop that ultimately influences our thoughts, and the way to improve is to get out of this vicious cycle. We must replace our negative thoughts with more positive ones, with the condition that the latter be realistic and not merely vain self-affirmations that have no backing or truth to them. The general process for our purposes is to observe, challenge, and replace negative thoughts and self-talk.
- One effective method to reduce negative self-talk is an activity called thought stopping. This involves distracting yourself from troublesome thoughts using some behavioral or mental cues, such as thinking or saying "Stop!", pinching yourself, etc. Though this technique can backfire in some cases, it has been observed to be effective in curtailing superficial but unproductive rumination.

- Besides using cues, other ways to stop negative self-talk include listening to music or podcasts that you like. This distracts you by engaging your auditory faculties. You can also use scattered counting— counting random numbers instead of proceeding linearly like in 1,2,3, and so on. The idea is to catch yourself in the process and distance yourself from unhelpful thoughts.
- If thought stopping doesn't work, you can also practice thought replacing. Here, you take a negative thought and strip it of all the components that make it unpleasant, replacing them with more positive alternatives. One way to do this is to simply think your thoughts through and assess how valid they are. If you find them to be irrational, substitute ones that make more sense to you and promote healthier emotions.

- Alternatively, you can write particular thoughts down to edit and rewrite them. Eliminate extreme words like only, never, absolutely, etc., along with any harsh descriptors like idiot, loser, ugly, and others. Also replace outright lies, unfounded assumptions, and other logical faults to improve your self-talk.

Chapter 5. The Emotional Immune System

Let's return to an example we explored in the last chapter: worrying about whether your spouse's family would judge you when they come to visit for the holidays. Let's be honest—there are indeed judgmental people out there in the world, and it's wholly possible that people may be unkind and unfair in their appraisal of you. However, let's imagine that you have judgmental in-laws but also have a rock-solid sense of self-esteem.

You notice them make a few disparaging remarks about the state of your sofa or that their TV is nicer, but instead of getting carried away with thoughts like "they think they're better than me" or trying to fight back by judging them in return, you don't react. You remind yourself that you are a good person and that you like yourself, that you have made choices that you're (largely) proud of, that you like your life and have plenty to be grateful for, and that even though you have some flaws and aren't perfect, you're doing your best and there really isn't any problem.

Or perhaps the in-laws were never judging you in the first place. With a healthy self-esteem, you are not overly sensitive to rejection and liable to imagine insults when there aren't any. You convey an attitude of being comfortable with who you are, and people respond well.

In either case, your self-esteem has acted as a kind of psychological immune system and helped you moderate the potentially damaging effects of negative thoughts, feelings, and behaviors. In just the same way as a strong immune system protects your body from attacks, your self-esteem will help you defend against undermining thoughts and feelings and behaviors that might work against you. In this case, instead of acting defensive and being icy with your in-laws, you're relaxed and friendly with them, avoiding all conflict and sparing yourself the stress of comparing your life to theirs.

When self-esteem (and not ego) is present, it determines how you feel about yourself, your self-talk narratives, and your baseline of resilience. Someone who feels good about themselves is even-keeled and calm, even in the face of failure, because they know they are a three-dimensional being with lots of positive traits and skills.

And of course, if you have higher self-esteem, your emotional needs are already more satisfied. Because you know what you need (side effect of heightened self-awareness!) and because you have faith in your own abilities to meet those needs, you're more likely to actually succeed in that regard. This also means that fewer things will trigger you, or at least it will take more powerful triggers to affect you.

Let's start with low self-esteem, and then we can work our way to healthy self-esteem. This is the feeling that you aren't good enough, that you are inadequate, that you'll be judged by others, and that others will reject you for being who you are. It's a feeling of constant insecurity in yourself and being terrified that others will agree with you. Many of our emotional needs and insecurities stem from this point—that you are somehow "less" than others. Not that you've done wrong, exactly, but that you *are* wrong. This creates an inevitable dynamic where you are always seeking to be accepted and seen as "equal" to others.

An example of this is a study by Keiichi Onoda of Shimane University in Japan. His study found that when our self-esteem is low, we experience rejection as more viscerally painful than when our self-esteem is high. Because of this, we withdraw from others and our confidence is diminished. Having good self-esteem not only gives you feelings of higher self-confidence, but also means that you will better be able to cope with certain pressures—your internal monologue turns from "I can't do it" to "I can handle this."

Low self-esteem also makes us more vulnerable to failure. We experience greater drops in motivation and have less perseverance after suffering setbacks or failures than those with higher self-esteem. It can also make us more vulnerable to anxiety and stress. Worse still are the results from a study conducted by Lupis, Sabik, and Wolf from Brandeis University. They found those who have lower self-esteem release a higher amount of cortisol, the stress hormone, into their bloodstream when they experience stress, and it stays there for a longer period of time. Low self-esteem quite literally makes you less emotionally stable. It truly functions like our real biological immune systems.

Another study led by Jeff Greenberg of the University of Arizona examined how people dealt with the anticipation of receiving a mild electrical shock. Half of the participants received an intervention that was aimed to improve their self-esteem, while the other half did not. Though they believed they were going to get shocked, no electrical shock was actually administered; it was only the expectation of it that was important. The results were clear: Those whose self-esteem was boosted showed significantly less anxiety than the others.

These findings all indicate that our self-esteem is responsible for not only our attitude and behaviors, but also the physiology of our bodies. Higher self-esteem means that common psychological problems such as rejection, failure, anxiety, and stress are easier to cope with. To put it broadly, self-esteem affects it all: our thoughts, behaviors, and feelings. It affects how we interpret neutral events and what we expect of ourselves, others, and life itself. It determines how we respond to setbacks and even the identities we give ourselves.

Therefore, boosting your self-esteem is probably one of the most effective and comprehensive ways to improve your overall resilience, emotional intelligence, and self-awareness. Think of it this way—none of the techniques outlined in this book or elsewhere have even a chance of working if they are poisoned by a firmly held belief in your own inferiority.

Now, our self-esteem also tends to have a baseline.

This is a general set level to which it commonly returns and is where people's resilience is based. The higher your baseline, the higher your emotional resilience. However, though there is a baseline, self-esteem is unstable enough that it fluctuates daily, if not hourly. To make things more complicated, our self-esteem is made up of not only how we feel about ourselves generally, but also how we feel about ourselves in specific areas of our lives—for example, as a parent, student, musician, or friend.

The more meaningful one of these areas is to us, the greater its impact on our overall self-esteem. If you are a professional chef and someone doesn't like the taste of your cooking, this will affect your overall self-esteem much more than it would affect someone who doesn't think cooking is a major aspect of their identity. Similarly, if you pride yourself on being a good parent and trying to do the best for your children, criticisms toward your parenting skills will affect you much more than other criticisms you may receive.

The extent that something will affect you is all about how important an area is to your overall identity. Knowing this means that you can understand why you are being affected by something and that you can better control your reaction and your self-esteem in response. Instead of feeling your self-worth plummet because someone doesn't like your meal, you can identify that it is important to you and instead ask them how to improve. Identifying the problem means that you have something to fix instead of just generalizing and thinking that you will never be able to succeed because of one criticism.

Mind Games

An important factor is the need to be realistic and set correct expectations. People change.

Self-esteem is useless if it is based upon a version of you that does not exist or no longer exists. Claiming that you were a certain weight in high school, that you could run so many miles when you were younger, or that you were once able to solve a particular calculus equation at one point in time isn't something that you need to dwell on. That's simply not who you are anymore, so always comparing yourself to that person is an exercise in futility.

You are different, and that's not necessarily negative. We all have skills that we pick up and lose as life goes on. Just because you used to be much better at something, or able to do it at all, doesn't mean you need to make comparisons to your past self. You may have lost some skills, but perhaps you've also gained some in the process. Today you may be a better cook than you ever were, a better writer, or more business-savvy than ever before.

For every skill or aspect you liked about your former self, another has taken its place that is equally praise-worthy. Don't sit around and reminisce about how you could once play the guitar really well. Value yourself on things that you are able to do right now. If it really means that much to you, you can very easily pick up the instrument and learn how to play again—most of us will never take this step, so it's clearly not that important to us and is used primarily to beat ourselves up via comparisons.

Evaluate yourself based on who you are at this very moment, not on some past version of yourself and not some future version that you believe you should be. Let go especially of some hypothetical version of yourself that you believe is the "real you." Your self-image should change and adjust constantly to match who you are and who you've become based on current abilities and skills. Adjust your beliefs about yourself so that they are realistic, and focus on your current strengths, goals, and aspirations. Think of the example of someone who has a closet full of clothing that doesn't fit them anymore. Perhaps you are the kind of person who has a closet full of clothes that never even fit to begin with, perhaps bought with a vague idea of the perfect person you thought you could or should or might be . . . but aren't.

But if you forget about all that and just meet yourself where you are, you will be accepting yourself for who you are, and your self-esteem will lift as a result. This is a mindset shift that takes some time to get your head around—we do *not* build our self-esteem by becoming "better," but by having the courage to accept who we are right now. Do you hold the unconscious belief that "sure, I'll love myself and have confidence . . . just as soon as I XYZ?" Recognize that this is a self-sabotaging belief and will lead to lower self-esteem, not higher.

We are always told when we are younger to stop comparing ourselves to others because we are all different and all have different paths, goals, and decisions in life. By the same principle, we should stop comparing ourselves to who we used to be or who we think we *should* be. By accepting who we are right now, we will be infinitely more satisfied in all aspects of our lives.

This stands in stark contrast to the perfection myth that some people pursue and whose self-esteem suffers as a result. Myths of perfection come from unrealistic and too-harsh expectations of ourselves. Rationally, we know that nobody is perfect, but we still hold ourselves up to ideals that we may never be able to reach. Buying into these myths of what is and isn't acceptable will only hurt you and the other people in your life. You are just setting yourself up to be inevitably disappointed when you realize you won't reach perfection.

Reality will almost always clash with ideals of perfection, and this may lead to a dissatisfaction that can never be fixed. Perfection is simply unattainable for any of us. This is something we need to accept. You're never going to be absolutely perfect. You're never going to have the perfect body, the perfect life, the perfect relationship, the perfect children, or the perfect home. Yes, despite what social media tells you! Even if you think you have a degree of perfection, there will always be someone with more of something or someone who is better at something.

Take hold of your accomplishments as you achieve them. Acknowledge them for their actual value. Stop devaluing your achievements by saying that you could have done better, that it wasn't entirely perfect, or even that it wasn't a big deal for you. Appreciate them for what they are: achievements in their own right.

It may help to keep a journal or a list of things that you accomplish each day as a reminder of all you can achieve. Everything from large triumphs to tiny victories. Not only will it lift your spirits when you have feelings of self-doubt, but it will inspire you to do more just so you can write more. You may choose to write daily or maybe even once a week or month. It doesn't matter how you choose to take note of your accomplishments, just that you do. Because small goals are easy and quick to accomplish, you will build momentum each time you achieve something and then strive to keep going.

Even better, consciously remind yourself to look for things that are *already good*. Sometimes, we put ourselves on a kind of treadmill—the moment something good happens to us, we quickly accept that as our new normal and start looking to the next step with dissatisfaction, failing to appreciate what we have. Can you think of all the things in your life right now that other people would be thrilled to have or experience? Can you see that there are in fact things about you that other people wish they could share, in the same way as you may be pining for someone else's life?

When something doesn't go perfectly, it's not a reflection of you. A key part of self-esteem is learning to differentiate between circumstances and your identity. Your circumstances are external events you may not have control over. You are not your mistakes. Your identity is not based on the last thing that you did or did not do successfully. It is more useful and effective to concentrate on things that you can change as opposed to things that you can't.

For example, perhaps you have decided you want to be more fit and healthy. You start eating healthy foods and exercising several times a week. You have changed your entire life around, banned all sugar from the house, and are only allowed healthy things. The problem is that one day you get a terrible craving and eat decadent chocolate cake instead of the healthy meal you were planning.

Before thoughts of failure kick in, or the feelings of inadequacy because you didn't successfully stick to your plan, take a moment to put things into perspective. Making one bad eating decision is not fundamental to who you are as a person. It should only be treated as a mistake that you will try to rectify, not as a sin that will forever mean that you weren't good enough. Remember the rest of your victories over the week or month. Instead of focusing on one decision that doesn't define who you are, focus on the decision itself. Perhaps you might rework your diet so that on occasion you may have food you love in smaller quantities that won't affect your overall health.

The key here is to focus on how to improve, not on what you think you've done wrong by not reaching perfection. Your self-esteem will improve if you focus less on your perceived failures and more on trying to strive for success.

It's clear that boosting our self-esteem can improve our emotional immune system. But how do we do this when our self-esteem is low? Isn't that like telling a slow runner to simply run faster if they want to improve their running?

One of the keys is to pursue activities that remind you of your self-worth. Identify something you're good at; perhaps it's cooking or maybe it is a particular sport. Once you have that activity in mind, make sure you allocate time to actually engage in these activities. Self-esteem is built up when you achieve and improve in areas of your life that matter. If you pride yourself on being a good cook, throw more dinner parties and try to perfect difficult recipes. If you pride yourself on being a good runner, try for a new personal best, sign up for races or marathons, and train for them. Identify your core strengths (everyone has them, even you) and find opportunities and careers that allow you to capitalize on them.

By focusing on your strengths and successes, self-esteem that was once restricted to certain domains will begin to transfer to the rest of your life. This will allow you to work on your weaknesses in privacy and safety because you will be firm in the knowledge that your strengths define you, not your weaknesses. When you feel good about what you can do, not what you can't, you can concentrate and remember these strengths in times of hardship.

Self-criticism is hard to ignore. We all want to be better and can't help but judge much of what we do too harshly, even if we wouldn't judge another for it. Even if it feels compelling or motivating, self-criticism is almost entirely useless. This is because you're focusing on the negative things instead of the positive. If your goal is to enhance your self-esteem, you need to substitute self-criticism with self-compassion.

To do this, any time your self-critical inner monologue kicks in, take a moment to consider the criticisms themselves. Imagine if a close friend was in the same situation. Would you have the same reaction? We tend to be far more compassionate to our friends than to ourselves. Think about what you would say to a friend in your situation and direct those comments at yourself instead. Doing so will avoid damaging your self-esteem further with critical thoughts. Instead, you will be able to build up your self-esteem and treat yourself less harshly as a result. This subtly speaks to the types of harsh and unrealistic (and perfectionistic) expectations you place on yourself and how damaging they are.

For example, imagine yourself trying to engage in a new hobby. Learning a new skill is always difficult, and you know this. However, you find yourself not showing even the slightest bit of improvement or success. Self-critical thoughts may begin at this point. It may not even be because you aren't very good at one particular activity. Often it may spiral into thoughts of every other thing that you may or may not be good at.

This is where you need to stop and take a step back. What would you say to a friend who was also struggling with one of their new activities? Chances are you'd probably say something much more positive, something about keeping motivation and practicing again and again until you succeed. You may feel like this is sugarcoating the issue a bit, but it's also the truth and not the worst possible interpretation of the events at hand.

Now direct that positivity at yourself and replace those negative self-critical thoughts you had before. You're only human and you're allowed to not be perfect. By giving yourself a chance to fail and by being okay with that failure, you're really giving yourself a chance to succeed and thus boosting your self-esteem.

The Self-Esteem Cycle

Why are some people able to roll with life's punches and come out on top, while others feel so much less emotionally robust and able to cope with adversity?

Many people fundamentally misunderstand the nature of self-esteem and where it really comes from. We might think that a high self-esteem comes as a reward for being "good enough" or that it's a state of mind that occurs when external elements recognize our worth and praise or reward us.

But self-esteem is an *inner* quality that is wholly independent from the external, even though it interacts and adjusts with reality. High self-esteem is not arrogance, nor is it the feeling of being immune to criticism or as though one is perfect. Similarly, high self-esteem doesn't mean we never encounter doubt or difficulty in life.

Simply, self-esteem can be better thought of as a *how* rather than a *what*. The practice of self-esteem is an ongoing cycle of behaviors, processes, and attitudes that we can strengthen and cultivate in everyday life.

It's never just one thing that makes you feel bad about yourself, and likewise, it's never just one thing that makes you feel more secure in who you are. The best way to see this in action is to look at the process as it unfolds in a person with a low self-esteem and then to compare it to what it looks like in a person with a healthier self-esteem.

Element 1: At-risk situations

An at-risk situation is any set of circumstances that directly challenges and threatens your unhelpful assumptions, core beliefs, and "rules" about life. The key here is that these situations are distressing precisely because they challenge our maladaptive beliefs about ourselves.

Consider a student who has the core belief of "I am not good enough." This forms a cluster of unhelpful "rules" that he has to follow, such as "I have to perform perfectly at school" or "I can never fail."

These are self-imposed rules, and as long as they are followed, the student feels okay about himself. His feeling okay is not true self-esteem, however, because the underlying core belief is still there, only hidden in a situation that doesn't trigger it. Should a situation develop in which the rule is broken and the assumptions threatened, this false sense of self-esteem will crumble.

The student may do poorly on a particular test (understandable, since nobody is perfect!) and immediately breaks his own unhelpful rule. This puts him at risk of low self-esteem since it triggers the core belief of "I am not good enough."

Element 2: Activation of unhelpful core beliefs

Notice that it is not the situation itself that is inherently causing the distressing feelings, but activation of the student's internal core belief. Similarly, the student can't be said to have high self-esteem outside of an at-risk situation—it only looks that way because his core beliefs have not been activated.

Examples of unhelpful core beliefs that can be activated:

"I am useless."
"I'm a bad person."
"I'm stupid."
"I can't cope with life."

Element 3: Developing biased expectations

So certain situations threaten to undermine our corresponding "rules" and then our core beliefs become activated. What happens next? If the rule has been bent a little but not exactly broken (for example, doing okay on a test but not exactly excelling), you may then develop an expectation of how the situation will further develop. This expectation is *biased* in the sense that it heavily favors a negative interpretation, one that confirms your negative core belief. You start to assume the worst and jump to unpleasant conclusions about the situation's outcome, seeing catastrophe everywhere.

The student in our example may make "predictions" such as "I'm going to fail this whole course," "the teacher probably thinks I'm an idiot," or "I bet everyone else is going to do better than me this year."

These negative predictions then push him to behave in corresponding ways. Perhaps the student starts to feel defeated and sabotages his studies by not trying too hard on the next test—this is escaping behavior. He may start procrastinating on homework and simply avoiding the looming deadlines he has—this is avoidance behavior. Alternatively, he might throw himself into over-studying, punishing himself with late nights—this is precaution-taking behavior.

Whichever route he goes for, though, they all leave him with a host of negative emotions. These negative emotions form a framework through which everything else is interpreted. But it can be a self-fulfilling prophecy: If anxiety about poor future performance actually damages those future performances, he might confirm the negative beliefs that led to that anxiety in the first place, creating a vicious cycle.

Without giving himself the chance to challenge these biased perceptions, they only become more and more concrete. He may "teach" himself to cling to escaping, avoidance, or precaution-taking behavior. Even when things turn out well, his biased expectations force him to interpret them badly. "I was lucky this time" or "this outcome was just a fluke; it doesn't mean anything."

Element 4: Developing negative self-evaluations

Alongside the building of biased expectations, he might simultaneously develop a negative perception of himself, especially if the "rule" he had was actually broken. If the student fails a test outright, he might be consumed with shame and self-criticism. Tried, judged, and executed in the court of his own mind, the student might berate himself and let those negative core beliefs run amok.

And just as with biased expectations, this inward assessment of his value as a human being causes certain harmful behaviors in response: retreating from life, self-harm, neglecting to take care of himself, giving up, or accepting poor treatment because he doesn't believe he deserves any better.

Element 5: Negative core belief is confirmed

By this point, low self-esteem is in full swing and may cause the student to feel depressed and extremely down about himself. Negative "self-talk" nurtures the harmful core beliefs, these beliefs bias expectations and self-evaluations, and these both cause the student to behave in ways that reinforce that core belief, starting the process over again. The belief is kept alive and current—"I'm not good enough"—even though the triggering event (doing poorly on an exam) has long since passed.

This is why so many people appear to have low self-esteem when to outsiders, they seem to be doing well in life—the original negative life experiences have passed. The person is *actively maintaining* feelings of worthlessness in the present with their thoughts and corresponding actions.

So you can see that self-esteem is not a fixed state of mind, but rather a complex mix of interacting thoughts, feelings, and actions that reinforce a negative underlying belief that one is, essentially, "bad."

Knowing how this process works and knowing that poor self-esteem begins with at-risk situations, we can take conscious control and deliberately work to reverse the cycle, curb negative self-talk, and begin to replace harmful core beliefs with more realistic, helpful ones.

Let's consider the same student who instead manages to halt the process of negative expectations and self-assessments. Let's look at how he might use knowledge of the model described above to foster a healthier, balanced state of mind when it comes to his studies.

Turning the low self-esteem cycle on its head

Again, imagine that the student does poorly on a test or fails it outright. These triggers threaten to undermine his "rules," and this then activates his core belief that he is not good enough. The experience of feeling his self-concept threatened in this way can serve as a flag for the student, alerting him that he is in a vulnerable position.

Here, he can pause and merely notice what he is feeling and thinking:

What emotion is looming on the horizon?
What thoughts and beliefs are behind this feeling?

What "rules" does he sense being broken or threatened here, and could this be activating a negative core belief?

A good way to get a handle on these processes is to write them down or keep a "thought diary." Take the time to notice when you are triggered and try to unpick thoughts and behaviors *before* they happen. Naturally, this is something that improves with practice.

Knowing how things could unfold, the student might choose to look more closely at his expectations and self-assessments. If he catches himself in self-talk that tells him how things are only going to end badly, he can recognize this and pin it down.

Is it strictly true that doing poorly on one test means you can't ever do well on another test again? Going deeper, is it really true that he has to perform perfectly every time or else? Going even deeper still, is it really true that he is not good enough?

By slowing the process down and shining some conscious attention on these processes, the student can give himself time to stop them and adjust as necessary. Similarly, he can notice when he is making self-assessments that are fueled by his negative core belief. He might write a mantra at the front of his notebook—"You are

a good person. You don't have to be perfect"—
and remind himself to read it again and again.

By changing his biased expectations and harmful self-evaluations, he gives himself the opportunity to then engage in behaviors that will help rather than hinder. Instead of withdrawing, avoiding, or taking precautions, he can take on his activities with an open, accepting mind and engage in new challenges with optimism. Without the baggage and momentum of low self-esteem, he can appraise each new situation afresh, approaching opportunities and trials without fear or resistance.

What's more, healthy behaviors like this will reinforce themselves with time, confirming a more helpful core belief—"I am a good person." Instead of getting caught in spirals of shame and self-blame, the student can recognize when he has behaved in adaptive, healthy ways. He can push himself to carry on studying and engaging with his schoolwork despite his previous test result. When negative thoughts and feelings come up, he can use the opportunity to reexamine and gently challenge his expectations, interpretations, and core beliefs. And when he behaves in healthy ways, he can stop and take the time to notice and reward himself.

Did he do better on the next test? It would be a good idea to reward himself—not for doing well on the test, but for getting closer to a healthier core belief. New core beliefs will only strengthen the more we can acknowledge them as evidence for alternative beliefs. Remember to "bank" these gains and recognize them for the growth that they represent.

Nurturing self-esteem means continually pausing to question beliefs you may have just assumed to be correct in the past. If you discover a "rule," prediction, or assumption about the world or yourself, stop and take a close look at it.

- Is this really an accurate portrayal of reality?
- What are the pros and cons of thinking/feeling/acting this way, and do you want these results?
- What impact do these beliefs have on how you behave and feel?
- Is there a way to adapt these beliefs so they're more realistic and helpful?

Doing so then gives you the chance to reconsider the behaviors that come from these thoughts, beliefs, and feelings. If believing that you are incompetent means you never try anything, the outcome will be a self-fulfilling prophecy. But if you deliberately decide that the most helpful behavior will be to actively engage with life despite uncertainty, you put yourself on a different path.

Instead of setting yourself up for more of the same, you open to new opportunities and experiences. You become more flexible, more responsive to life, and better able to learn. You may or may not find yourself adjusting unhelpful rules and assumptions, but you at least give yourself the opportunity to question them, immediately empowering yourself and confirming your ability to take control of your own self-esteem. Every time you approach a new at-risk situation, you are strengthened and better able to cope.

Again, we can see that healthy self-esteem is not a single behavior or feeling but an ongoing series of feelings and behaviors. Individuals with healthy self-esteem

- have realistic expectations of themselves, others, and the world that are not overly biased
- have self-evaluations that are not filled with blame, condemnation, or judgment
- choose those behaviors that are most helpful and adaptive to them
- have core beliefs that are reasonable and open to adjustment with further evidence

- have rules and assumptions about life that do not result in negative self-evaluation or biased expectations

Overall, a person with high self-esteem can manage even challenging situations because they have unshakeable core beliefs that they are worthy. They do not make external circumstances a condition for their own self-acceptance.

A student with a healthy self-esteem is able to say, "I did poorly on this test. I'm not happy about it, but that's okay. I don't have to be perfect all the time. I'll try to understand what I didn't get right the first time around and will do my best on the next test. I trust myself to figure it out. Through challenges and difficulties, I'm still a good person. No matter what."

Takeaways:

- Self-esteem is the emotional immune system because it insulates you from emotional triggers, needs, and pains. The person who generally feels positively about themselves is not prone to emotional instability or reactivity because they simply aren't affected in the same way.
- Like the external world, our identities are entirely neutral, and self-esteem is a lens we view ourselves through. This means we have

the power to see ourselves however we want, and for some of us, this is terrible news. A primary reason is an unreasonable set of expectations about yourself, the world, and your place in it—you will never live up to these expectations, so you can literally only fail in your mind, which makes you feel even worse than before.
- Self-esteem, as with many things about emotions, is not living in a vacuum and is best understood as a cycle of causes and effects. We begin with inaccurate assumptions and arbitrary (and disempowering) rules about life that are confirmed through inevitable failure. Then our narrative begins to include this data point and creates an increasingly negative self-evaluation. The inaccurate assumptions and beliefs are then strengthened, and it becomes even more difficult to climb out of this pit of despair. Deciphering these beliefs and seeing them nullified by reality is key.

Chapter 6. Preventative Care

As we've discussed and you have no doubt noticed from your own life, the brain maintains a strong negativity bias. This is just the way it is—like having a house that constantly gets dirty and needs to constantly be cleaned. Life is filled with challenges, unknowns, and other people's decisions that affect us whether we like it or not. While we all know we should tidy the house, brush our teeth, and clear our inbox every day, how many of us make conscious efforts to do "psychological housekeeping" to make sure we're staying on top of potential negativity?

Our continued survival depends on our ability to keep harmful elements at bay as much as possible—dangerous encounters, food one is allergic to, toxic people or situations to avoid, and so forth. But because neural activity in response to negative signals is so strong, it can cease being an effective survival mechanism and become an obstacle to your emotional stability and overall happiness.

We've gone over many techniques and tools for keeping it together and even-keeled in the face of emotional triggers and feelings of impending doom, but what about the everyday ways in which this negativity bias affects us? Part of the battle in staying even with your emotions is to actively battle this instinct and generate your own positivity.

To a lot of us, that's no small task. Negativity is more accumulative than positivity, piling up in the psyche with seemingly little effort. It's easy for the brain to lie back and let fears, terrors, and anxieties unfold one after the other. When they get to a certain mass, negativity bias starts to feel like an anchor that can't be overcome.

That is, unless we *deliberately constantly make the choice to cultivate positivity.* This is important: It doesn't happen by itself, in just the same way as your house won't clean itself!

We tend to characterize positivity as something that requires more labor, an exhaustive act that might not even make a significant dent in our negativity in the end. But in reality, positivity is a force that pays off even when we take small steps to bring it about. It's far easier to inject positivity into our lives and emotions than our negativity would have us think.

Improving your emotional response and coping mechanisms will always be effective. But for everyday life, it's best to have some strategies that aren't necessarily developed in crisis mode. Taking preventative measures will keep you healthy and grounded and form a solid foundation that eases the strain of emergencies.

Write It Out

Keeping journals is a part of almost any facet of modern life you can think of—business, art, information-gathering, and, of course, news. It's not a stretch to understand its service in the maintenance of ourselves and our mental health—we've already covered how it can help you bring awareness to your gratitude and savoring practices. A couple more journal techniques are particularly helpful in your quest for emotional calm.

"Worry journals" are an element of cognitive behavior therapy (CBT), a long-time aid in treating emotional disorders. They've also been used in sleep therapy for subjects who experience anxiety. The goal of the worry journal is to air out our worries, fears, anxieties, and issues on paper throughout the course of the day.

One method of worry journaling involves writing one's concerns or fears on the left-hand side of a page, thinking about how to resolve them, and writing these plans on the right-hand side. The writer then closes the journal and at least tries not to think about the worries until the next day when, theoretically, some of the plans can be executed.

Researchers from Pennsylvania State University decided to see whether worry journaling alone could improve the emotional balance of subjects. They recruited fifty-one patients with various forms of anxiety disorder. From this pool, certain subjects were randomly selected to keep a worry journal for ten days. Those remaining were told to keep a journal in which they simply recorded their thoughts. The researchers also text-messaged participants at random times during the day, prompting them to write immediately.

After the ten-day experiment ended, those with worry journals were asked to review how many of their worries had actually come true. Most of them (ninety-one percent) hadn't. The brief text interventions were enough to significantly reduce their anxiety levels, more so than those who had simply kept thought journals. Thirty days after the experiment concluded, the worry journal group still performed better than the control group.

An interesting finding of the Penn State study was how quickly the worry journal participants manifested positive changes, even after only ten days. By documenting their worries, fears, obstacles, and predictions, they made progress in reorienting themselves in the present—not the future where some of their biggest anxieties lay. There appeared to be a light at the end of the tunnel, and people weren't just spiraling into the worst-case scenarios. "It may also make the worthlessness of engaging in excessive catastrophic expectations more apparent," the researchers said.

These results support the idea that putting our self-inventories on record can be effective in managing stress. Worry journaling can be a beneficial part of your regular response to stress and daily routine. For example, let's say that your business has lost its biggest customer or that you've had a contentious argument with an employee. In frustration, you walk into your office and shut the door. Your emotions aren't controllable—you're upset, angry, and maybe even frightened of the fallout.

To regain your emotional balance, you focus on your breathing for a few moments. Then you open your journal. You write down exactly what's upsetting you; what you're worried about; and what your biggest obstacles, problems, or fears are. You must be honest—understand that nobody except you will read this journal unless you give it to them.

Some experts suggest writing in your journal every single day. That's certainly not a bad idea, but sometimes life intrudes upon our ability to do that. We don't always have time. Other days, we *do* have time but don't feel like we have anything significant to say. But in moments of worry, anxiety, or upset, we *always* have something to say—and plenty of it. Keeping it bottled up may prevent us from doing anything else until we finally express our frustrations, so that's a good reason to write it down in the journal on the spot.

These situations illustrate a good practice when it comes to journaling: *follow your emotional prompts.* Writing during times when we're scared, angry, or upset might not be the first action you'll think of taking, but it can go a long way in addressing your immediate emotional needs. By the time you're done, you might be at least a little glad you did, and chances are good that the next time, writing *will* be the first action you take.

The journal is where you dump your frustrations, problems, and concerns. Keep writing until you've finally written everything you need to say. Remember, the journal's a "safe zone" and you're not obligated to share it with anyone. It's where you can be direct, unsparing, and honest without unforeseeable repercussions. Once you express these feelings and get them out of your system, you no longer feel that you are burdened by them internally.

Two outcomes will probably emerge from documenting your feelings. While writing, you'll gradually become calmer and less upset. You may start to see solutions to your problems come forth. Laying out your problem in words on the page makes a future course of action appear and helps you figure out what to do.

Journaling is free-flowing and open-ended, but another approach that could be helpful involves making two lists that are very specific in what they accomplish.

"Stop" and "It's Okay To" lists serve as daily affirmations of your values. They remind you what's acceptable and what's not, what boundaries you have set up, and what brings you closer to your goals. They're also empowering—they give you self-generated, unequivocal directions. "Stop" items are things you should hold yourself back from; "It's Okay To" items list out what's acceptable.

Write out these lists and post them in a place you see regularly. They'll serve as guidelines that will keep you on course to a life of emotional strength and wellness. See the following example:

STOP:	IT'S OKAY TO:
Putting yourself last	Ask people for help
Trying to be all things to all people	Be constantly changing
Being afraid to say no or yes	Admit vulnerability and weakness
Talking down to yourself	Not be impenetrable
Talking and not listening	Be knocked down and feel hopeless
Depending on others to make you happy	Cry
Letting outside events define you	Speak up for what you value
Settling for less	Take time to determine your feelings about a situation
Limiting beliefs	Always be in "learning" mode
Keeping score in games you don't need to—or can't—win	Question the rules of the games you do play

After making these lists, we can incorporate their contents into internal action when we have a conflict. Since they are based on the values *we* define for ourselves, the hope is that these principles will be easier to stick to when such a situation arises.

For example, someone in your extended family comes to you with an investment opportunity. They've had a difficult time staying afloat as an adult and have been bailed out once or twice after making some unwise credit decisions. You mistrust their judgment about financial matters. But since they're family, you let them talk to you, and you listen completely to their pitch.

While they seem earnest about the opportunity, you have doubts that it's anything more than a pyramid scheme, and you say so. The family member becomes angry and accuses you of being closed off to new ideas and "going against the family." You attempt to explain your position more patiently, but before you finish, they angrily stomp out. As a result, you feel some amount of guilt and shame.

Let's use the above "Stop/It's Okay To" lists to back up your reactions (your personal lists may be different, but for this example, we'll use ours). Your instincts told you to reject your family member's latest plan, and they responded negatively. One of the "Stop" items is "Being afraid to say no." Perhaps you have a tendency to help as many of your friends or family as you can, which is impossible to fulfill. But another "Stop" item is "Trying to be all things to all people." In this scenario, you've successfully prevented those acts from happening.

What about the "It's Okay To" list? In a patient manner, you explained your reasons for not agreeing to invest. That could answer a couple of items on the "It's Okay To" list: "Speak up for what you value" and possibly "Take time to determine your feelings about a situation." You explained why taking on this dubious investment goes against your needs and principles, but only after you also let them finish so you could hear them fairly.

After the conflict ended, you might have felt guilty or ashamed. But you acted according to the ground rules you set forth in that list, which are completely reasonable and come from your own self-questioning. Knowing that you stuck to your self-defined principles may not make you feel better *immediately*—but probably much sooner than you would have if you *didn't* stick to them.

Again, your personal list will likely vary from our example. You should have some items unique to your own experience, and that's what makes the lists invaluable. Mistakes, regrets, and even accidents can happen when we forget or work against our belief systems and values. These lists are one way to keep them near the forefront of our attention, and though they won't eradicate all conflict from our lives, they could help us navigate them with more assurance.

Brain Dumping, Mental Noting, and Scheduled Worry Time

Chris had trouble navigating annoying and irritating life obstacles.
Carrie had to challenge the distorted mental filters she was using to look at herself.
Dan battled to reframe the story of guilt and shame he was living inside.
Ellen struggled to step outside of her depression and low mood.

And Alex had to learn to cope with the very real limitations of physical pain.

Each of these people had to deal with very different problems, but ultimately, each of them worked through their own version of negative thinking and how to find a way out of it. There is one manifestation of negativity that we haven't yet considered, though, and that's anxiety. This chapter is for you if you find your negativity taking the shape of worry, rumination, overthinking, and stress.

In the spirit of radical acceptance and not fighting against our mind or against reality, we'll begin with **a basic CBT principle when dealing with anxiety: We are not attempting to force**

ourselves not to worry. It's just like being told "don't think of a pink elephant." Merely saying it makes you think of a pink elephant! So, first things first: getting anxious about your anxiety and worrying about your worry is not going to get you anywhere.

Instead, tap into the capital letter You and remind yourself that you have a choice. In the technique of "worry postponement," we essentially tell ourselves, "Okay, Mind, you have full permission to worry. I'm not stopping you. All I'm going to do is decide *when* you get to do it and for how long." In fact, tell yourself that your intention is to **worry more efficiently**. So, for example, you decide that instead of worrying right this instant, you're going to deliberately worry later tonight at 6 p.m. for twenty minutes.

Scheduling your negativity and worry may seem like an odd thing to do, but it works. This is because
1. You're learning to be aware that you are in fact worrying. (Again, it's about gaining distance—it's not, "Money's tight!" but, "I'm having a stressful thought about money right now.")
2. You avoid getting tangled up in that worry but also avoid going to war with it, resisting it, or denying it.

3. You take control. Just because a thought pops up and says, "Look at me!" it doesn't mean you have to obey.
4. You gain a deeper sense of how worry actually plays out in your life—how it comes and goes, rises and falls, and in time, how utterly useless it usually is . . .
5. You put yourself in a proactive state of mind where you stop worrying and start *strategizing*.

Anxiety is exactly the kind of mental activity that, if not engaged with, will eventually dissipate. You can probably think of a few things you were really worried about a day or a week or ten years ago, and which barely even register with you now. Why? Simply because some time has passed.

When you schedule your worry to take place some other time, you may notice how often you actually forget about it when the allotted worry time rolls around. Or, when the time comes and you have free rein to worry to your heart's content, you realize that the issue just doesn't seem that important anymore. Sometimes, when you arrive at your future worry appointment, you discover that you don't even *want* to worry anymore, that you are feeling way more calm and able to deal with any negativity that remains, or that the negativity has already resolved by itself.

Here's how worry postponement might look in practice.

Be Mindful
You're noticing a recurrent them here, right? It all starts with simply being aware that you are having anxious thoughts and worries in the first place. Just perceive and observe; don't judge. Try not to be too hard on yourself if you notice a worry spiral that seems to be getting out of hand. Try to practice a little radical acceptance.

"I'm feeling extremely worried and anxious at the moment."

"I am feeling so on edge. My stomach's in knots."

"I keep having the thought *what if* and am having trouble stopping it."

Postpone
Even if you have to do it out loud, give yourself permission to worry; only, the worry has to be deferred to a time of your choosing. Make sure that the time you choose is at least a couple hours away (to give your mental state time to change) but not so far off that you unconsciously feel like it won't really happen. Write down
- the day, date, and time,
- the duration for the worry,
- what you will worry about.

For example, let's say you're worrying about an upcoming performance review at work. You notice your anxious overthinking: *"Maybe it'll be really embarrassing. What am I going to do if they keep talking about the incident in March? It may be that they've already discussed it amongst themselves already. Maybe everyone has discussed it, and they're getting ready to fire me at this very moment. What if I cry or get angry during the meeting? What if I say something I regret...?"*

You stop and become mindful and realize that your anxious thoughts are getting carried away. You say out loud, "That's okay, but we're not worrying right now." In a notebook, you scribble down "11 a.m. Tuesday, ten minutes worry time, concerns about upcoming performance review." Then you close the notebook. You've made an agreement with yourself, and so you don't have to keep worrying.

Follow Through
Naturally, your mind will soon start up again with worries. "Do you think you should maybe prepare a few clever rebuttals for if they want to talk about what happened in March? Just in case?" You notice this, and you don't argue with it. You also don't act or respond in any way. "No, Mind, we aren't doing this now—we're worrying tomorrow at 11 a.m., remember?"

Actively remind yourself that the big important issue your brain is trying to draw your attention to will certainly get the attention it deserves ... in due course. Tell yourself that you're allowed to focus on the present moment's tasks because the worry is actually taken care of for now. All the time from now until 11 a.m. tomorrow is now "free." When the thought pops up, confidently tell it, "Oh, don't worry, I've already dealt with you!"

What about when 11 a.m. comes around? Well, do as you said you would and sit down and worry for ten minutes. But really worry! Don't let your mind wander to *other* worries—just the one you said you'd tackle. You may as well really go for it because once the ten minutes are up, you're not going to think about it anymore. Notice what happens when you do this. You might

1. no longer care about this problem,
2. feel better able to cope with it or manage it,
3. realize an action you can take to fix it,
4. still be at square one with no solution in sight.

Almost always, the outcome will be 1, 2, or 3. Occasionally, though, you will chew over something, and it will still be bothering you. Try your best to ask if there is one small thing you can do, there and then, to improve the situation. Then schedule that in, and promptly forget about it. If you catch yourself worrying further—then repeat the process. Postpone that worry till another time. At the very least, you are limiting your exposure to a difficult situation that you cannot do anything about.

You might start to notice that you keep worrying about something that either a) never comes, or b) does come and isn't as bad as you thought it would be, or even c) it does come, it *is* that bad, and it doesn't matter because you were able to cope with it.

One variation of this practice is to externalize worries while you're postponing them. So whatever pops into your mind, imagine that you're redirecting it to the page and writing it down there. The rule is, once it's written down in the worry book, it does not need to be in your head anymore. The worry book is like a repository. All through the day, collect little nagging fears and concerns as they crop up and put them aside to mull over later, on your own terms.

After a while of doing this, ask yourself a few questions:

Are there any recurrent themes?
How often does the thing you fear actually come to pass?
Is there any difference in outcome when you do worry versus when you don't?

A final variation is called "brain dumping," and it's exactly what it sounds like. When it's your scheduled time to worry, go all out and put

EVERYTHING down on the page. You can rant, you can rave, you can say what you like and let it all out. For five whole minutes (try not to go too much longer than this!), you have no limits and can experience the full cathartic power of worrying as hard as you can worry.

Imagine that your brain is like a room in a house that has just become too cluttered with junk. When you do a brain dump, you're basically throwing all this clutter out. The power lies in acknowledging the thoughts and putting them outside of yourself. A big reason we worry is because our brain thinks it's being useful. It wants to keep drawing our attention to something that may be threatening or a problem in the future, but if you put it down on paper, this sends a strong message to your unconscious mind: "I've noted this. It's being dealt with. I won't forget. You can stop reminding me now!"

What should you include in your brain dump? Whatever you need to. Scribble down stream-of-consciousness ideas, thoughts, feelings, and fears. Put down things you're worried about forgetting on your to-do list. Regrets, concerns, complaints—anything you like.

What you do with your brain dump from there is up to you—the wonderful thing is that once it's out on paper, you can do something about it. Here are a few options:

- Burn, crumple, or throw away the paper if what you've expressed is just useless or destructive material. Breathe a sigh of relief.
- Process what you've written. Pick one thing that's bugging you and consciously decide to take a step to address it. Just one thing, though—you can't tackle it all!
- Go through the material, identify negative and self-defeating beliefs, and gently rewrite them. Turn them into affirmations that you begin the following day with. The ABC method described above can be a great technique to incorporate here.
- If it makes sense to you, pray about or meditate on some of the things that are weighing on your heart but you're stuck with. Ask a higher power to help you carry the burden, or do a visualization exercise where you release yourself from having to worry about it anymore.

Turning Anxiety into Mindfulness
People who struggle with anxiety are actually blessed with a secret superpower. If they harness it, they are able to tap into an enormous potential for heightened conscious awareness. Every intrusive and anxious thought can be like

a "meditation bell" calling you to awareness and bringing you back into the moment. How?

Try "mental noting." It's easy.

1. Become aware and observe yourself having thoughts. No judgment.
2. Note the experience and label it. "I'm thinking."
3. Keep going. Repeat until the thought dissipates or you move on.

Every time you have a thought, any thought at all, you can stop and remember to become aware of yourself. In some Buddhist temples and monasteries, a mediation bell rings periodically so that wherever people are and whatever they are doing at that moment, they can stop and reconnect to the present again. You can do the same with your own thoughts and self-talk. Every time you hear an anxious thought, treat it as a bell that has rung to remind you to come back to the present.

Of course, you won't be able to maintain awareness one hundred percent of the time, but if you can grab hold of an anxious thought and note it for what it is, then you can transform *any* thought into an opportunity to be mindful.

This technique is inspired by many different mediation techniques and is designed to quell distractions and calm down what the Buddhists call "monkey mind"—that inner chat that thoughtlessly leaps from one thing to another. Mental noting might not seem like much, but if you pepper your day with little moments of metacognition in this way, be prepared for big, big changes in the long run. Practice this often enough and you will find it much more difficult to become "fused" with negative thoughts. You simply maintain too much distance to ever get too tangled up.

Just remember three key elements when you practice mental noting:

Your **intention** should be to maintain awareness of the present moment.
Your **attention** should be on everything that is happening in the present only.
Your **attitude** should be non-directional, non-judgmental, and kind.

The classical approach during mediation is to say, for example, "There is hearing," or, "Hearing has happened," when you notice a dog barking outside. You might be really Zen and simply note, "Hearing." You don't allow yourself to run off and follow the hearing so that you are soon thinking, "That's the neighbor's dog," or, "I wish it would shut up." You simply note and label what your brain is doing, then move on.

In the case of anxiety, you do something similar to stop yourself from getting "distracted" by thoughts that seem urgent and important but really aren't. So if you're sitting at your desk, trying to work, and you notice a thought pop into your mind ("The performance review is going to be so awkward!"), you stop in your tracks, note the thought, label it, and move on without engaging. "Ruminating," you say, and pass it by.

Another way to bring in the principles of mindfulness to a brain that's hooked on anxiety is called "mundane task focusing." If you're one of the many people who dislike meditation or simply don't find room in their lives to practice it, don't worry—the Buddhists and meditators do not have the monopoly on mindfulness!

All that's required to calm an anxious mind is to remain in the moment. Anxieties and worries live *elsewhere*—they're in the past or the future. If you anchor right here and right now, though, your world slows down and becomes calmer and way more manageable.

1. Pick a mundane and everyday task that doesn't require too much brainpower—for example, washing dishes.
2. Do the task but do it very intentionally. Pay ultra-close attention to what you are doing. Focus on the bubbles of the soap.

The temperature of the water. The rhythmic movement of your hands, and the weight of each dish as you hold it (as you can see, this is a form of grounding).
3. When your mind wanders, pull it back to the task at hand. Commit every last ounce of your attention to the task unfolding before you, nothing more.

You can find immense relief from overthinking and worry by doing completely ordinary everyday tasks, like walking to the post office or filling the car with fuel.

Boundary Defense

You're on your way to work and an aggressive person handing out pamphlets in the street gets in your way, forcing you to politely but firmly say no. You get to work and are asked to chip in to a company fundraiser for charity—despite the fact that you have already contributed hundreds this year alone. You graciously say no to this as well. That annoying colleague who sits two desks down from you walks over during lunch and launches into a big rant about her ex-husband. To stop from becoming her free daily therapy, you politely excuse yourself. At the canteen, you spot that one server at the till who is always playfully forcing you to have one more scoop of potato salad on your plate despite your protests. Today, you avoid them entirely and stand in another line instead . . .

Preventative care is important, but what might be even more important is to train yourself to defend against those who are actively trying to undermine your emotional resilience and actually prefer you unstable. This is when you must proactively establish self-defense from others, whereas the rest of this book has been about defeating your own demons and defending against yourself. For our purposes, this comes in the form of defending your boundaries.

That people don't always behave as we'd like is a hard lesson to learn in all relationships. Seeing apathy, carelessness, or a lack of respect for others' feelings is a great source of stress and unhappiness. Trying to modify others to act and feel in ways we prefer is an exhausting and futile exercise. This is simply because it's a battle we can never win! There will *always* be someone who wants to talk over you, twist your arm, or try to get you to agree to more than you're comfortable with. It's sadly a fact of life.

All we *can* do is adjust ourselves and what we accept from others. We demonstrate our capacity for love, communication, support, and inspiration as best as we can and in ways we hope can be perceived. In others, we seek affirmation, or at least recognition, of our best efforts. In rare cases, we may find those whose ideals closely mirror our own. But ultimately, other people do what they're going to do, and we either accept them for who they are or walk away from them.

However, there's an element of relationships that you have more control over than you may think. It's a healthy kind of control that respects your values and feelings and reinforces your balanced relationships with others. That element is *setting and keeping emotional boundaries.*

This doesn't mean devising a list of ultimatums that other people must live up to, or risk losing your friendship. Neither does it mean erecting a wall around your emotions or feelings in overprotection. What boundaries *do* mean is making sure that you are caring for yourself first and foremost. They keep you happy, healthy, and emotionally balanced.

Boundaries in healthy relationships are strong and scrupled but flexible enough to respond to altered circumstances and each party's own uniqueness. They support each member's efforts to live full lives while developing legitimate respect, trust, and support over a long period of time. Setting up boundaries is an introspective and practical process, and occasionally, people will tell you that your boundaries are wrong. They might be right, but subjective boundaries also exist.

Define your limits. Be honest with yourself about the point where others' behavior crosses your personal lines for acceptance and safety. What subjects are you sensitive to no matter how objectively silly they might sound? At what level does someone's voice go from concern to anger? What makes you comfortable, and what makes you anxious?

Monitor your feelings. "Trusting your gut" is certainly a key thing to do when you're confronted with an immediate situation. But pay close attention to how you're reacting in social or low-pressure circumstances as well. If a conversation's taking a turn that makes you uncomfortable, mark that point and ask yourself what could be causing your stress. Being self-aware in itself isn't a sign of narcissism or selfishness—it's a basic survival mechanism. Your annoyance, discomfort, or guilt is the red flag that your boundaries are being stomped on.

Set a communication plan. Very few of us talk or act the same way with every single person we know (if we do, that's probably a problem). But in close relationships, at some point the need to discuss our boundaries will arise, and you should make a plan in advance for how you will communicate your feelings. Being direct is always the preference, but the definition of our relationship is important in figuring out how to express that directness. In personal relationships, we might feel free to speak openly and ruminate. In professional or complicated situations, we may need to be level and determined.

Keeping up a sense of self-awareness, as mentioned, is a key part of relationship health. Being truthful about the effectiveness of our internal boundaries—and taking proactive, corrective measures when they fall short—is crucial to this honesty. It also goes a very long way in protecting oneself from the operations of emotional manipulators.

Even if we know and set our emotional boundaries, we may overlook them in practice with others or not always recognize when our boundaries are being trespassed. Since emotional manipulators thrive on blurring those boundaries and resetting them to reflect their own interests, developing a keener sense of when those trespasses happen is extremely useful.

For obvious reasons, it's easier to notice verbal violations. Any effort to invalidate or disparage you or your emotions should be evaluated in relation to your boundaries. These include someone not allowing you to speak or be heard by silencing or talking over you, screaming, making derogatory statements about your integrity, or even flat-out gossiping about you in plain sight. Violations of your psychological and emotional boundaries can be more difficult to spot and harder to quantify. They could include the following:

- preying on your self-esteem
- using things you've said to them in confidence against you
- lying
- criticizing, demeaning, and judging
- making fun of you or your thoughts, feelings, and beliefs
- making you feel guilty or responsible
- demanding your time and energy
- shaming and embarrassing
- bullying
- claiming their thoughts and beliefs are superior to yours

While defining and setting up boundaries is the important pivot point in any relationship, maintaining them is equally essential. Psychologist Dana Gionta identified two key feelings that should be red flags that we're letting go of our boundaries.

Discomfort. "When someone acts in a way that makes you feel uncontrollable, that's a cue to us they may be violating or crossing a boundary."

Discomfort can arise from triggers about past issues or traumas, someone communicating in an overly frantic or antagonistic way, or being in an unexpected or unsafe situation. It can also simply arise from being put in a position where you feel interpersonal tension.

Resentment. This usually comes from being taken advantage of or not being appreciated. We feel that someone else is imposing their expectations on us. Resentment can arise when we're asked to fix an ongoing series of crises, when we get left out of important work decisions after habitually working overtime, or when we simply don't get anything back from what we give.

Gionta recommends gauging our feelings on a scale from one to ten and sounding the alarm if our intensity goes higher than six. When that happens, she suggests asking what's causing the feelings and what about the situation is bothering you.

Frequently, the root impetuses are fear, guilt, and self-doubt. We fear others' responses when we set and keep our boundaries. We feel guilty if we speak up or say no. And we doubt that we even deserve to have boundaries in the first place.

What we have to remember is that boundaries are key signs of a healthy relationship and vital steps toward self-respect. You're the exclusive owner of your own feelings, and as their protector, you have full permission to set and preserve your emotional boundaries. But knowing where you stand is a necessary measure in deciding your boundaries. Identify your limits: physical, emotional, mental, and spiritual. Concentrate on what you can tolerate and what you can't accept. "Those feelings help us identify what our limits are," Gionta says.

Take time to consider your present social circle and close friendships. Think about whether your give-and-take is healthy and whether the relationships are truly reciprocal. If you notice a certain behavioral strain or commonality with your friends (or with yourself), address it in your investigation, whether good or bad—it could help detect further clues about your emotional realities.

Finally, examine how your daily environment outside of relationships could be impacting your health. Your work environment is a good place to start. For example, if your workday is supposed to be eight hours but your coworkers regularly stay at least ten or eleven, is there an unspoken mandate that you're supposed to go "above and beyond"? How does your office cope with sudden emergencies or long-term conflicts?

Keeping boundaries intact is a solo exercise—it springs from your own personal observations and experience. It can be challenging, especially if somebody feels they're the only one trying to maintain boundaries. But it's a regular way to tend to our feelings and needs and a good mechanism to remind ourselves how we need to honor them.

Takeaways:

- What is preventative care in the context of mastering your emotions and keeping calm while the world spins on? It is recognizing the fact that our brains have an intense negativity bias, even while things are going well and we aren't on the brink of disaster. And thus, we should seek to immunize our resilience through daily actions.
- Writing your feelings down in a journal is not an uncommon piece of advice. It is the act of expressing yourself and then being able to introspect later on. Most of us miss these two important steps, and our emotions remain pent up and unable to develop and unfurl. Of particular use is writing down all your worries and then writing down solutions for them. Also, you can write down two distinct types of lists: "Stop Doing This" (something

detrimental) or "It's Okay To" (something beneficial).

- With anxiety, our goal is not to force ourselves not to worry, but to worry more efficiently. Scheduling worry time puts you in proactive control and helps you gain distance.
- Notice the anxiety, write down the time you'll postpone to—with the duration and content—then follow through as agreed. Mental noting and focused mundane tasks can help you turn anxious moments into opportunities for mindfulness.
- Finally, come to the defense of your boundaries. This book has talked about how to deal with yourself—but what about others? After all, people are probably our strongest emotional triggers, and they hold enormous power over us. The best step for this is to understand boundaries. Most of your negative spirals with others are related to boundaries, so we must see the warning signs, set boundaries, and enforce them. Any set of negative feelings probably means that your boundaries are being violated in some way.

Summary Guide

CHAPTER 1. OUR VOLATILE EMOTIONS AND WHY THEY REIGN SUPREME

- Our emotions have enormous power over us. Sometimes this is good, and other times, it makes us feel completely out of control. This is bad. But there is good reason for this type of power—you can view emotions as a type of warning signal that has evolved alongside humans to keep us alive and healthy. In the absence of higher critical thinking, emotions taught us about the world and how to regard it. This is also the reason that negative emotions can make us spiral out of control so quickly.
- These types of dangers aren't present anymore in our modern lives, and our task now is less survival and more controlling and harnessing our emotions. The extent to which we do this can wholly determine how our lives go. In no way is this suggesting that emotional suppression is the key to happiness. In fact, emotional suppression is linked to poor health outcomes, so we must simply find the fine line of healthy emotional expression and reaction.

CHAPTER 2. THE KEYS TO ELIMINATING EMOTIONAL TRIGGERS

- When we talk about emotional resilience and calm, we are really talking about the emotional triggers that push us over the edge. The vast majority of the time, these triggers will be subtle and external and not at all proportionate (or even related) to the response they will create within you. This is the classic case of overreacting to a simple statement based on how it made you feel, not the actual substance.
- Of course, this is because our emotional needs are being exposed, poked, or prodded in an uncomfortable way. To escape this discomfort, we react by lashing out, avoiding, or coping in a variety of other ways. Very few of these habits are healthy, and this sequence of events is what will lead to your unraveling and emotional instability.
- It's not enough to simply know your emotional needs; we need to gain emotional granularity into what is actually happening. A doctor can only treat a sickness if they know the actual cause, and Plutchik's wheel of emotions is a useful tool in labeling yourself and escaping the uncertainty of a general feeling of dread and discomfort. In fact, diversity of emotion helps us remain balanced and even-keeled.

CHAPTER 3. RECOGNIZE, RESPOND TO, AND REGULATE THE CHAOS IN YOUR BRAIN

- Now that we've got an understanding of emotional triggers, needs, pain, and how they all interact with each other, we must talk about how to deal with them. How can we inject self-awareness into our lives, recognize what's happening, and keep the volcano (us) from erupting? The first model to think about is responding versus reacting. When we touch a hot stove, we react without thought, instinctually, and protect ourselves. This is rarely necessary from an emotional standpoint, and yet we find ourselves similarly volatile to a volcano instead of pausing a beat to think and then respond.
- Next, we should think about a framework for regulation that plays with the emotional triggers and needs we have discussed. This consists of selecting the situation (avoiding triggers), modifying the situation (decreasing triggers), shifting focus (ignoring triggers), changing thoughts (changing the trigger), and changing response (reacting less to a trigger).
- This leads directly to the next point of distress tolerance. Sometimes we are indeed too prone to flying off the handle; we are

overly sensitive in a way that makes us unpredictable and fragile. Thus, we need to work on increasing our tolerance to distress and anxiety. This has common elements with the framework for regulation, but it focuses more on foregoing the comforting escape mechanisms you use and staying in the situation and emotion. The purpose is to accept anxiety and distress, withstand the major emotional spike surrounding it, and stay with it until it subsides and you realize that you are still doing fine.

CHAPTER 4. FIGURING OUT AND REPLACING YOUR EMOTIONAL PATTERNS

- Our lowest emotional points don't exist in isolation; they almost all exist due to various cycles of triggers, emotional needs, behaviors, and then consequences—all of which strengthen the cycle for the future. So it's necessary to cut the cycle short and interrupt it in any way that we can. The most valuable way we can do this is through simply analyzing how it takes place in our lives.

- The first tool for this is the ABC Loop, which stands for antecedent, behavior, and consequence. They generally describe the main elements of an emotional outburst that we can break down and analyze: What happens before, what you did to cope, and what happens afterward that makes the cycle even harder to escape.

- The second tool is similar but more in-depth: emotional dashboarding. It describes the same cycle but through a different lens, with elements of situations, thoughts, emotions, bodily sensations, and impulses/actions. This gives you an even deeper view into certain situations and why you felt the need to lash out or become dragged down by negativity. The important thing to keep in mind with both of these tools is that the willingness for deep honesty is required.

- CBT is a popular and effective therapeutic framework that emphasizes our thoughts as the key component of our feelings and behavior. The underlying principle of its techniques is that our thoughts influence how we feel, which in turn determines the way we behave. This creates a feedback loop that ultimately influences our thoughts, and the way to improve is to get out of this vicious cycle. We must replace our negative thoughts with more positive ones, with the condition that the latter be realistic and not merely vain self-affirmations that have no backing or truth to them. The general process for our purposes is to observe, challenge, and replace negative thoughts and self-talk.

- One effective method to reduce negative self-talk is an activity called thought stopping. This involves distracting yourself from troublesome thoughts using some behavioral or mental cues, such as thinking or saying "Stop!", pinching yourself, etc. Though this technique can backfire in some cases, it has been observed to be effective in curtailing superficial but unproductive rumination.
- Besides using cues, other ways to stop negative self-talk include listening to music or podcasts that you like. This distracts you by engaging your auditory faculties. You can also use scattered counting— counting random numbers instead of proceeding linearly like in 1,2,3, and so on. The idea is to catch yourself in the process and distance yourself from unhelpful thoughts.
- If thought stopping doesn't work, you can also practice thought replacing. Here, you take a negative thought and strip it of all the components that make it unpleasant, replacing them with more positive alternatives. One way to do this is to simply think your thoughts through and assess how valid they are. If you find them to be irrational, substitute ones that make more sense to you and promote healthier emotions.

- Alternatively, you can write particular thoughts down to edit and rewrite them. Eliminate extreme words like only, never, absolutely, etc., along with any harsh descriptors like idiot, loser, ugly, and others. Also replace outright lies, unfounded assumptions, and other logical faults to improve your self-talk.

CHAPTER 5. THE EMOTIONAL IMMUNE SYSTEM

- Self-esteem is the emotional immune system because it insulates you from emotional triggers, needs, and pains. The person who generally feels positively about themselves is not prone to emotional instability or reactivity because they simply aren't affected in the same way.
- Like the external world, our identities are entirely neutral, and self-esteem is a lens we view ourselves through. This means we have the power to see ourselves however we want, and for some of us, this is terrible news. A primary reason is an unreasonable set of expectations about yourself, the world, and your place in it—you will never live up to these expectations, so you can literally

only fail in your mind, which makes you feel even worse than before.
- Self-esteem, as with many things about emotions, is not living in a vacuum and is best understood as a cycle of causes and effects. We begin with inaccurate assumptions and arbitrary (and disempowering) rules about life that are confirmed through inevitable failure. Then our narrative begins to include this data point and creates an increasingly negative self-evaluation. The inaccurate assumptions and beliefs are then strengthened, and it becomes even more difficult to climb out of this pit of despair. Deciphering these beliefs and seeing them nullified by reality is key.

CHAPTER 6. PREVENTATIVE CARE

- What is preventative care in the context of mastering your emotions and keeping calm while the world spins on? It is recognizing the fact that our brains have an intense negativity bias, even while things are going well and we aren't on the brink of disaster. And thus, we should seek to immunize our resilience through daily actions.
- Writing your feelings down in a journal is not an uncommon piece of advice. It is the act of expressing yourself and then being able to

introspect later on. Most of us miss these two important steps, and our emotions remain pent up and unable to develop and unfurl. Of particular use is writing down all your worries and then writing down solutions for them. Also, you can write down two distinct types of lists: "Stop Doing This" (something detrimental) or "It's Okay To" (something beneficial).
- With anxiety, our goal is not to force ourselves not to worry, but to worry more efficiently. Scheduling worry time puts you in proactive control and helps you gain distance.
- Notice the anxiety, write down the time you'll postpone to—with the duration and content—then follow through as agreed. Mental noting and focused mundane tasks can help you turn anxious moments into opportunities for mindfulness.
- Finally, come to the defense of your boundaries. This book has talked about how to deal with yourself—but what about others? After all, people are probably our strongest emotional triggers, and they hold enormous power over us. The best step for this is to understand boundaries. Most of your negative spirals with others are related to boundaries, so we must see the warning signs, set boundaries, and enforce them. Any set of negative feelings probably means that

your boundaries are being violated in some way.

www.ingramcontent.com/pod-product-compliance
Lightning Source LLC
Chambersburg PA
CBHW020529080526
44583CB00013B/793